DK Pocket Genius

HUMAN BODY

FACTS AT YOUR FINGERTIPS

Written by Richard Walker

DK DELHI
Project editor Bharti Bedi
Project art editor Isha Nagar
Senior editor Samira Sood
Senior art editor Govind Mittal
Assistant editor Neha Chaudhary
DTP designers Jaypal Singh Chauhan, Pradeep Sharma
Picture researcher Sakshi Saluja

DK LONDON
Senior editor Fleur Star
Senior art editor Rachael Grady
US editor Margaret Parrish
US senior editor Rebecca Warren
Jacket editor Manisha Majithia
Jacket designer Laura Brim
Jacket manager Sophia M. Tampakopoulos Turner
Production editor Rebekah Parsons-King
Production controller Mary Slater
Publisher Andrew Macintyre
Associate publishing director Liz Wheeler
Art director Phil Ormerod
Publishing director Jonathan Metcalf

First American Edition, 2013
This edition published in the United States in 2016 by
DK Publishing, 345 Hudson Street, New York, New York 10014

A catalog record for this book
is available from the Library of Congress.
ISBN: 978-1-4654-4588-9

DK books are available at special discounts when purchased in
bulk for sales promotions, premiums, fund-raising, or educational
use. For details, contact: DK Publishing Special Markets,
345 Hudson Street, New York, New York 10014
SpecialSales@dk.com

Printed and bound in China

A WORLD OF IDEAS:
SEE ALL THERE IS TO KNOW
www.dk.com

CONTENTS

Being human

The human body has unique features that have enabled us to become the most successful animals on the Earth. We are the most intelligent and we have special ways of moving, communicating, and staying warm.

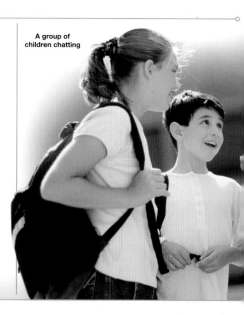

A group of children chatting

On two legs
Humans stand on two legs, which allows us to walk or run long distances. Being upright raises the head, letting us see farther, and leaves the hands free for tasks such as using tools.

In touch

Being able to talk to people using spoken language is unique to humans. It helps us to make and maintain social relationships. Other animals do this with calls and body language but not with words.

Skillful hands

Human hands are incredibly flexible and can perform a wide range of movements. The thumbs and fingers can grip precisely for delicate tasks such as painting, or grip powerfully to pull a heavy weight.

Keeping warm

Humans are the only animals that wear clothes. This way of keeping warm allowed early humans to migrate from tropical Africa, where they first appeared, to colder climates, including the Arctic.

Body builders

The human body is made up of trillions of microscopic cells. Each cell is a living unit with a complex structure. Inside each cell are even smaller structures called organelles that control, produce, and move materials, release energy, and work together to keep the cell alive.

Inside a cell

Although cells come in many shapes and sizes, they all share the same basic structure. Each cell has a membrane, or outer layer, that surrounds the cell. Inside the membrane is a liquid, called cytoplasm, which supports all the different organelles.

Lyosomes recycle worn-out organelles

The **nucleus** is the cell's control center

Cytoplasm is a jellylike fluid that contains organelles

An organelle called the **Golgi complex** prepares proteins for use inside and outside the cell.

Structure of a typical cell, showing organelles

The **cell membrane** forms the cell's outer layer

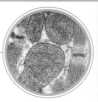

Mitochondria are the cell's powerhouses. They release energy, which is used to power the cell's activities.

Endoplasmic reticulum stores and transports proteins that are made by tiny ribosomes (shown as purple dots) on its surface.

Microtubules are rods that support and shape the cell

Types of cell

There are around 200 different types of cell in a human body, each with its own job to do. Cells of the same type work together in groups called tissues. The size and shape of cells are linked to the specific roles they perform.

Cell variety

The six types of body cell shown here all have very different shapes and roles. For example, thin nerve cells carry signals over long distances, allowing the brain to communicate with other parts of the body, while round adipose cells store fuel.

Red blood cells travel around the body in the blood. They are small and, unlike other cells, do not have a nucleus. They give blood its red color and carry oxygen from the lungs to all other cells.

Axon terminal transmits signals to the next neuron

Epithelial cells are tightly packed together and form a protective barrier that stops germs from invading body tissues. They cover the skin and line hollow organs such as the mouth and lungs.

Adipose cells contain a large droplet of fat—one of the body's sources of energy. These cells also help insulate the body.

Nerve cells, or neurons, carry electrical signals and make up the brain, the nerves, and the rest of the nervous system—the body's control network.

Axon, or nerve fiber, carries signals

Dendrites pick up signals from other neurons

Muscle cells shorten, or contract, and pull to create movement. In addition to moving the body, they also push food along the intestines and make the heart beat.

Photoreceptor cells are sensitive to light and are found inside the eye. When light hits these cells, they send signals to the brain that allow us to see.

Dividing cells

We all start life as a single cell. That cell divides again and again to produce the trillions of cells needed to build a body. Without cell division—or mitosis—the body would be unable to grow. It would also be unable to repair itself by replacing worn-out, damaged, or lost cells.

Identical offspring

In mitosis, a cell divides to produce two identical cells. Inside its nucleus, chromosomes hold the instructions to build and run the cell. First, each chromosome copies itself. Then, the two-stranded chromosomes line up. Next, the two strands are pulled apart to opposite ends of the cell. Finally, the cytoplasm divides to form two new, identical cells.

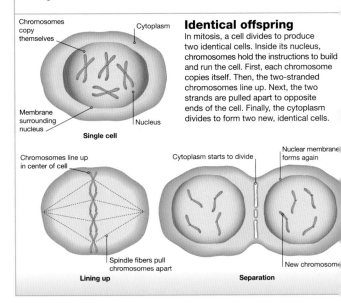

Chromosomes copy themselves

Cytoplasm

Membrane surrounding nucleus

Nucleus

Single cell

Chromosomes line up in center of cell

Spindle fibers pull chromosomes apart

Lining up

Cytoplasm starts to divide

Nuclear membrane forms again

New chromosome

Separation

Getting bigger

Humans grow from birth to their late teens, mainly as a result of cell division. Controlled by the body's growth hormone, cell division increases the number of cells, allowing the body to grow. When growth ceases in adulthood, cell division maintains and repairs body tissues.

HEALING

If the skin is cut or grazed, the damage is repaired automatically. Cell division is an important part of this repair process. At the wound site, cells divide to produce new skin cells to replace those that have died or been scraped away. Cell division also plays a key part in repairing damage inside the body.

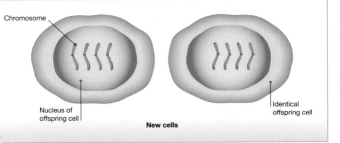

Chromosome

Nucleus of offspring cell

Identical offspring cell

New cells

From cells to systems

The 100 trillion cells that make up the body do not operate independently of each other. If they did, the body would be an uncoordinated, shapeless mass. Instead, they are precisely organized to form tissues, organs, and systems that work together to make a complete, functioning human body.

Body organization

The body is organized as a series of different levels. At the lowest level are cells. Cells work together in groups called tissues. Different tissues are grouped together to produce organs, such as the heart. At the highest and most complex level, organs are linked together to form a system, such as the circulatory, or blood, system.

CELL

TISSUE

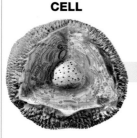
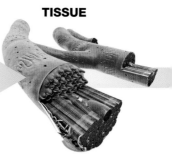

This typical **cell** shows the features that are common to all cells. Cardiac muscle cells, with these and other features, are found in the heart. They contract, or shorten, to make the heart beat.

Cells of the same type work together in a group called a **tissue**. Cardiac muscle cells are linked together in a network to form cardiac muscle tissue.

SYSTEM

The heart is a **powerful pump** located in the chest. It pushes blood along a network of blood vessels to all parts of the body.

ORGAN

Organs, such as the heart, are made of two or more types of tissue. In addition to muscle tissue, the heart also contains connective tissue, which holds it together.

Like other **body systems**, the circulatory system is made up of organs that are linked together. These include the heart and blood vessels through which a liquid tissue—blood—flows.

Looking inside

Years ago, the only way doctors could look inside a living body was by cutting it open. Today, they can use many different techniques to produce images of body organs and tissues without causing any harm. Some of the most common methods include X-rays, CT scans, MRI scans, and ultrasound.

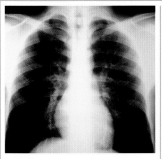

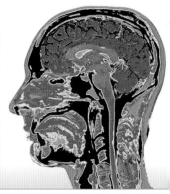

MRI scan

The scan below shows a cross-section through the head and was produced by magnetic resonance imaging (MRI). A person lies inside a tunnel-like scanner and is exposed to powerful magnets. This causes body tissues to give off radio waves, which the scanner's computer turns into images.

X-ray

Discovered in 1895, X-rays are a form of high-energy radiation. These rays are beamed through the body onto a photographic film. Hard body parts, such as bones, absorb X-rays and show up clearly on film. X-rays pass through soft tissues, so these are less visible.

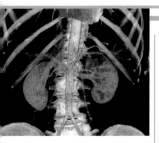

Ultrasound

High-pitched sound waves are used to create ultrasound images, such as this one of a 20-week-old fetus (unborn baby). Sound waves bounce off the fetus, creating echoes that are turned into images by a computer.

CT scan

A computed tomography (CT) scan is produced by sending beams of X-rays through the body and turning them into "slices" through organs and tissues on a computer. These slices can be built up to produce 3-D (three-dimensional) images, such as this one of the abdomen.

Endoscopy

An endoscope is a thin, flexible tube with a camera at one end. This is inserted into the body so that doctors can see on a screen what is happening.

SEM

Using a special type of microscope, scanning electron microscopy (SEM) produces magnified, 3-D images of tissue samples taken from the body. This SEM image shows plump adipose cells taken from the layer of fat under the skin.

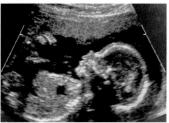

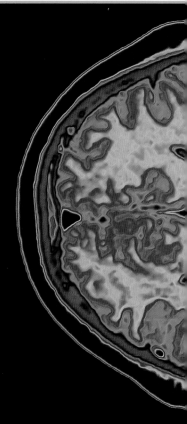

The human brain is about the size of a cauliflower, but weighs

3 lb (1.4 kg)

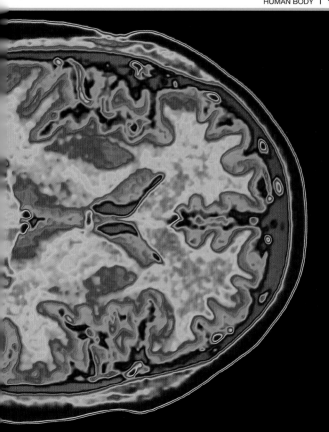

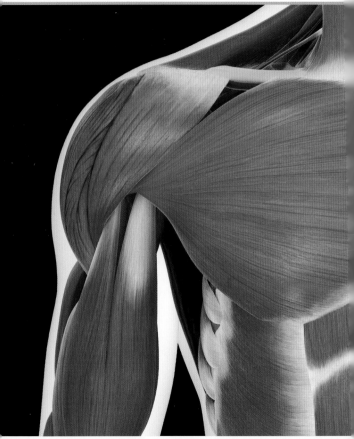

Shaping the body

Together, the skeletal system, the muscular system, and the skin support, shape, move, and cover the body. The bones of the skeletal system form a structure that is strong enough to support the body's weight, but light and flexible enough to allow it to move. The muscular system works with the skeleton to shape the body, and, by pulling bones, makes the body move. Skin provides a protective overcoat around the whole structure.

SMALLEST BONES
The three ossicles are the body's smallest bones. The tiniest ossicle is the size of a grain of rice. They are linked together and found in the ear, where they transmit sounds.

Skin

The largest organ in the body, the skin forms a barrier between the body's insides and the outside world. Waterproof, germ-proof, and self-repairing, the skin also screens out harmful rays from the Sun and allows people to feel their surroundings.

Skin-deep

The skin has two layers. The upper, protective epidermis consists mainly of flattened cells packed with keratin, a tough, waterproof protein. Below that, the thicker dermis contains blood vessels, nerves, sweat glands, and other structures.

Sebaceous glands release sebum, an oily substance that softens the skin

Hair follicles are narrow pouches from which hair grows

Arteries supply food and oxygen to skin cells

Nerves carry signals from the sensors to the brain

Sweat glands release sweat

New skin

The epidermis is made up of different layers of cells. The top layer of dead cells is constantly worn away and replaced by new cells that move upward, flattening and dying as they do so. In this way, the skin regenerates itself.

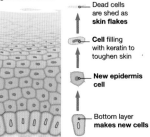

Dead cells are shed as **skin flakes**

Cell filling with keratin to toughen skin

New epidermis cell

Bottom layer **makes new cells**

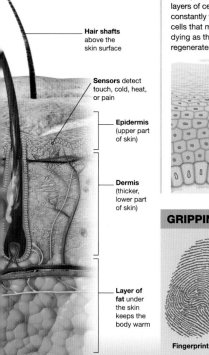

Hair shafts above the skin surface

Sensors detect touch, cold, heat, or pain

Epidermis (upper part of skin)

Dermis (thicker, lower part of skin)

Layer of fat under the skin keeps the body warm

GRIPPING RIDGES

Tiny ridges at the end of each finger help the fingers grip objects. On hard surfaces, such as glass, these ridges leave behind sweaty patterns called fingerprints. Each person's fingerprint patterns are unique.

Fingerprint

Hair and nails

Both hair and nails grow from the skin. They are made from dead cells packed with tough keratin. Hair covers most parts of the body. Nails protect the sensitive tips of our fingers and toes and help us to grip small objects.

Hair structure

Each flexible strand of hair grows out of a follicle. Hair consists of a shaft that appears above the skin's surface and a root below it. At the base of the root, new cells are produced that move upward and make the hair grow. The hair onv your head grows about ¹⁄₁₀₀ in (0.3 mm) each day.

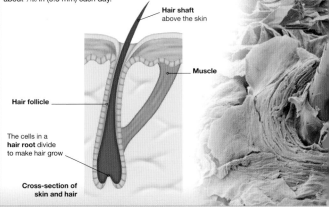

Hair shaft
above the skin

Muscle

Hair follicle

The cells in a **hair root** divide to make hair grow

Cross-section of skin and hair

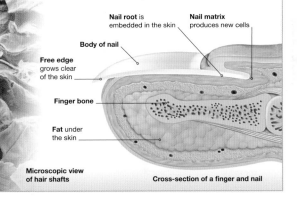

Body hair

The body is covered with millions of hairs. Thick terminal hairs, such as those of the scalp and eyebrows, help to protect the body. Shorter, finer vellus hairs cover much of the rest of the body.

Terminal hair

Vellus hair

Protective nails

Each nail has a root and a body, and ends in a free edge. In the nail matrix behind the root, living cells multiply and push the nail body forward to make the nail grow. Most nails grow about 1/100 in (0.3 mm) each week.

Nail root is embedded in the skin

Nail matrix produces new cells

Body of nail

Free edge grows clear of the skin

Finger bone

Fat under the skin

Microscopic view of hair shafts

Cross-section of a finger and nail

Keeping warm

Skin plays an important role in keeping the body temperature balanced at 98.6°F (37°C), no matter how hot or cold it is outside. This is the ideal temperature for the body's cells to work at their most efficient.

Losing heat

Body cells produce heat as part of their everyday activities. This heat is lost from the body mainly through the skin. A thermal image, or thermogram, shows how the rate of heat loss differs for different body parts. The warmest parts of the image are light yellow, while the coldest are black.

Our body temperature drops slightly at night, by about 1°F (0.5°C), and rises slightly by day.

**Thermal image
of a boy eating
an ice pop**

Feeling hot

There are two ways the body loses heat to maintain its temperature in warm conditions. Tiny droplets of sweat released onto the skin's surface evaporate, drawing away heat and cooling the body. Blood vessels widen, increasing blood flow through the skin so that more heat escapes through the surface.

Hair lies flatter

Sweat droplet

Blood vessels widen

Skin responses to hot conditions

Feeling cold

When we feel cold, sweat glands produce little sweat and blood vessels get narrower. Both actions reduce heat loss from the body. Hairs are pulled upright, producing goosebumps on our skin.

Hair stands upright

Blood vessels narrow

Skin responses to cold conditions

Skeletal system

Without the bony framework of a skeleton, a person would collapse. The skeleton supports and shapes the body and protects vital organs. It works with the muscles to produce movement and also stores energy-rich fat and the calcium we need for healthy teeth and bones.

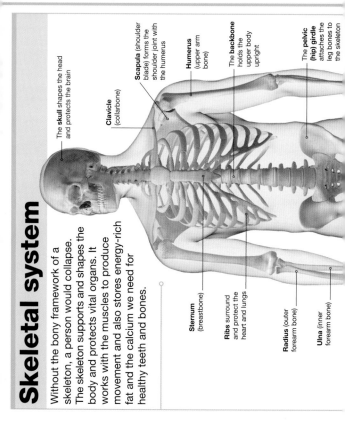

The skull shapes the head and protects the brain

Scapula (shoulder blade) forms the shoulder joint with the humerus

Clavicle (collarbone)

Humerus (upper arm bone)

The backbone holds the upper body upright

The pelvic (hip) girdle attaches the leg bones to the skeleton

Sternum (breastbone)

Ribs surround and protect the heart and lungs

Radius (outer forearm bone)

Ulna (inner forearm bone)

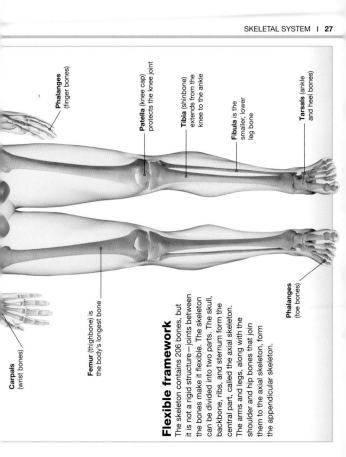

Phalanges (finger bones)

Patella (knee cap) protects the knee joint

Tibia (shinbone) extends from the knee to the ankle

Fibula is the smaller, lower leg bone

Tarsals (ankle and heel bones)

Carpals (wrist bones)

Femur (thighbone) is the body's longest bone

Phalanges (toe bones)

Flexible framework

The skeleton contains 206 bones, but it is not a rigid structure—joints between the bones make it flexible. The skeleton can be divided into two parts. The skull, backbone, ribs, and sternum form the central part, called the axial skeleton. The arms and legs, along with the shoulder and hip bones that join them to the axial skeleton, form the appendicular skeleton.

Weight for weight, bone is

five times stronger

than steel

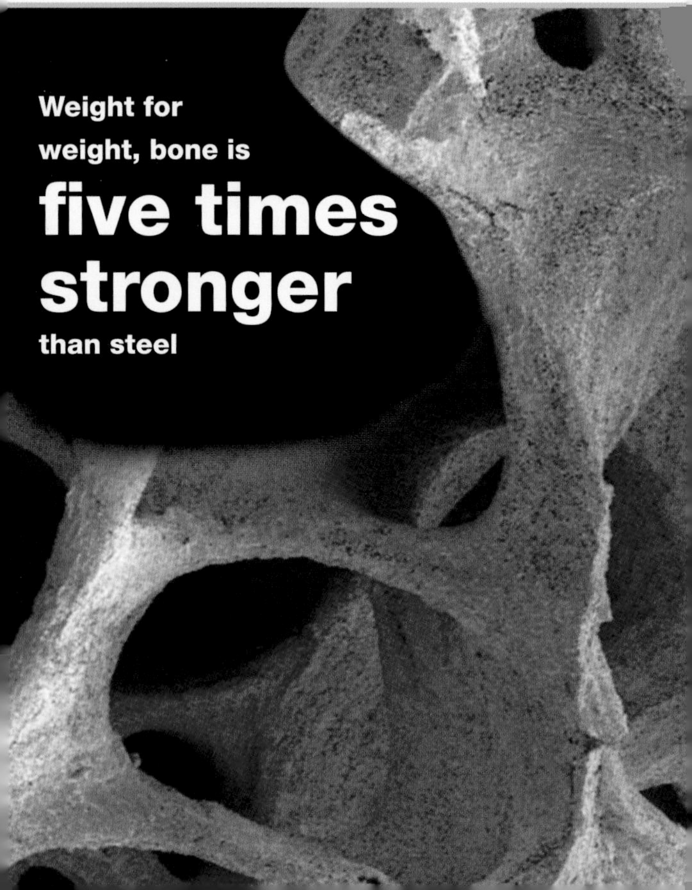

BONE TISSUE
This microscopic view inside some spongy bone shows a latticework of struts and spaces. This honeycomb structure makes the bone very light and incredibly strong.

Inside bones

Bones are made up of different types of bone tissue. In the outer parts of the bone the tissue is dense, but in the inner parts it is lighter. This combination makes bones strong enough to support weight but not so heavy that the body cannot move.

Structure of a bone

The view inside a bone shows its structure. The outer layer of hard, heavy, compact bone is made of tiny, bony tubes called osteons. It encloses lighter spongy bone. A central cavity contains yellow bone marrow.

Blood vessels supply bone cells with nutrients and oxygen

Epiphysis is the rounded end of the bone

Spongy bone is not squishy, as its name may suggest. It consists of a network of bony struts that make it strong but light.

Osteons give strength to compact bone

Yellow bone marrow filling is a fat store

Bone shaft connects the two ends of the bone

This microscopic section shows the osteons that run the length of the bone and make up the hard layer of **compact bone**.

Red bone marrow, shown here in blue, is a soft tissue that fills the spaces between the struts in spongy bone. It produces billions of blood cells every day to replace the ones that wear out.

Bone types

The shape and size of a bone depend on the functions it performs. Bones are divided into five different types, based on their shape—long, short, irregular, flat, or sesamoid.

Long bones

These bones are so named because they are longer than they are wide. This group includes most arm and leg bones, such as the body's longest bone, the femur, as well as the much smaller phalanges—the toe and finger bones. Long bones support the body and allow it to move freely.

Temporal bone

Femur

Short bones

Shaped roughly like cubes, short bones are found in the wrists and ankles. They do not allow much movement, but do help to support the hands and feet.

Wrist bones

Frontal bone

Flat bones

Thin, flattened, and usually curved, flat bones protect the body's most important organs. For example, the skull's temporal, frontal, and other flat bones surround the brain. Other flat bones include the ribs, shoulder blades, breastbone, and hip bones.

Irregular bones

These bones have complicated shapes. They include the 26 vertebrae that are stacked up to form the backbone or spine. In addition to supporting the upper body and allowing it to bend, the backbone also protects the spinal cord.

Vertebra

Spinal cord

Backbone

SESAMOID BONES

These bones are shaped like sesame seeds. The patella (kneecap), which is a sesamoid bone, is found inside the tendon that attaches the thigh muscle to the shinbone. It increases the muscle's pulling power and protects the knee joint.

Patella

Healing fractures

Bones are strong, but sometimes they fracture or break. When this happens, a self-repair mechanism springs into action. This process may need outside help from doctors to ensure that the bones—especially the arm and leg bones— are kept straight while they heal.

Healing in progress

This step-by-step sequence shows how a long bone heals. When a bone fractures, the body's immediate response is to stop bleeding from the bone's blood vessels. In the days and weeks that follow, new tissues are laid down that reconnect the broken bone ends. A broken bone can take months to heal completely.

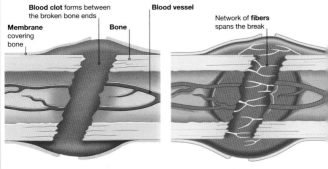

IMMEDIATE RESPONSE
Blood leaking from torn blood vessels forms a jellylike clot. This seals off the vessels and stops blood from pouring into the wound.

THREE DAYS LATER
Repair cells called fibroblasts move to the fracture and produce fibers made of collagen (a protein that works as a building material). These fibers connect the broken bone ends.

OUTSIDE HELP

Broken bone ends are usually held together in the right position to make sure they heal correctly. This is often done using a rigid **plaster cast**.

For more severe fractures, **pins** are used to keep the bones lined up. This X-ray shows pinned leg bones just above the ankle.

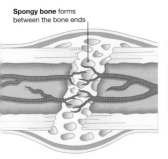

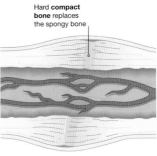

Spongy bone forms between the bone ends

Hard **compact bone** replaces the spongy bone

THREE WEEKS LATER
Bone-building cells are now active. They weave a mesh of spongy bone that provides a bond between the bone ends. But the bone is still weak and would be set in a plaster cast.

THREE MONTHS LATER
Blood vessels reconnect across the break. The healed bone shaft, made of compact bone, is almost the same shape as it was before the fracture.

How joints work

A joint is formed wherever two or more bones meet. Most joints, such as those in the fingers, are synovial joints. These allow the bones to move freely and give the skeleton its flexibility. Other joints, such as the semimovable and fixed joints, provide stability to the skeleton.

Flexible joint

This view inside a synovial joint shows how it works. The bone ends are covered by slippery cartilage and separated by oily synovial fluid. Together, these allow the joint to move easily and smoothly. A tough capsule holds the joint in place.

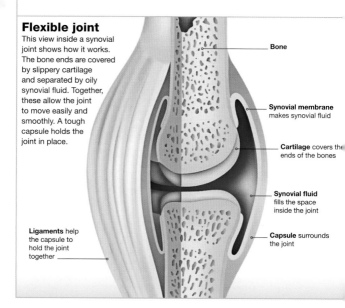

Bone

Synovial membrane makes synovial fluid

Cartilage covers the ends of the bones

Synovial fluid fills the space inside the joint

Capsule surrounds the joint

Ligaments help the capsule to hold the joint together

Held together

Many synovial joints, including those in the ankle and foot, are held together by tough straps called ligaments. Made from extra-strong collagen fibers, these allow the joints to move, but stop the bones from being pulled apart.

Leg bone

Ankle bone

Ligaments hold the bones together

Heel bone

Dislocated finger joint

Out of joint

This X-ray shows how two finger bones, forming a knuckle joint, have been pulled apart. This is known as dislocation and occurs when a sudden blow or pull forces the bones out of line. Doctors treat dislocations by moving the bones back into their correct positions.

Types of joint

There are more than 400 joints in a human skeleton. Most of these are the synovial (movable) joints that allow us to run or shake our head. Others are fixed, or permit only limited movements.

Movable joints

There are six types of movable joint in the body. Each type allows a different range of movement, shown here by arrows. Which way the bones can move depends on how their ends fit together in the joint. For example, the ball-and-socket joint in the hip allows the leg to swing in most directions.

Saddle joint allows the thumb to move freely and touch the other fingers.

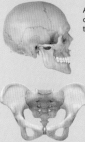

OTHER TYPES

All 22 skull bones, except one in the jaw, are locked together by **fixed joints**.

Semimovable joints, such as those between the vertebrae in the backbone and between the hip bones shown here, allow limited movement.

Ellipsoidal joint in the knuckles and wrists allows up-and-down and side-to-side movements.

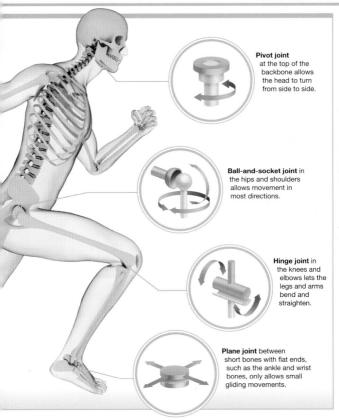

Pivot joint at the top of the backbone allows the head to turn from side to side.

Ball-and-socket joint in the hips and shoulders allows movement in most directions.

Hinge joint in the knees and elbows lets the legs and arms bend and straighten.

Plane joint between short bones with flat ends, such as the ankle and wrist bones, only allows small gliding movements.

Muscles and movement

Without the body's muscles, we would not be able
to move. The cells that make up the muscles have a
unique ability to contract (get shorter) and pull. Skeletal
muscles, for example, pull the bones of the skeleton
to produce an incredible range of movement, from
kicking a ball to scratching an itch.

Skeletal muscles

Layered over the skeleton, skeletal muscles
contract when they receive instructions from
the brain. Some skeletal muscles are large
and powerful—the bulkiest is the gluteus
maximus, which pulls the thigh back as
we walk, run, and jump. Others, such
as the finger muscles, are built for small,
precise movements such as turning a
page. Skeletal muscles not only move
the body, they also hold it upright.

Gluteus maximus,
or buttock muscle,
pulls the leg back
to straighten
it at the hip

Achilles tendon
links the calf
muscle to the
heel bone

There are more than
640 skeletal muscles
in the body, making
up nearly half of
its weight.

Thigh muscle
straightens the
leg at the knee

Calf muscle bends
the foot downward

Jaw muscle opens
and closes the mouth

Neck muscle bends
the head forward

Chest muscle pulls
the arm forward and
toward the body

Biceps muscle
bends the elbow

Abdomen muscle
bends the body
forward

Bone links

Muscles are linked to the bones they
pull by strong cords called tendons.
Tendons contain tough collagen fibers
that give them great strength. The end
of each tendon is embedded in the
outer layer of bone to anchor the
muscle firmly in place.

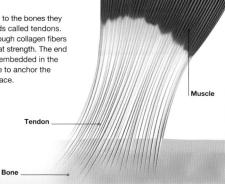

Muscle

Tendon

Bone

Types of muscle

There are three types of muscle in the body. Skeletal muscle pulls the bones, for example, when we walk. Cardiac muscle makes the heart pump blood. Smooth muscle pushes food along the digestive system and urine out of the bladder, among other functions.

Body movers

The skeletal muscles attached to our bones are under our conscious control. When we decide to make a movement, our brain instructs the right muscles to contract, or shorten.

Skeletal muscle fibers look striped under the microscope. Their overlapping filaments, or strands, work together to make a muscle contract.

Heart beater

Cardiac muscle is found in the wall of the heart. It contracts automatically thousands of times a day to make the heart beat. Without us being aware, signals from the brain speed up cardiac muscle contraction when we exercise and slow it down when we rest.

Cardiac muscle is made up of a branching network of interlocking fibers. This passes on the signals for the fibers to contract and produce a heartbeat.

Organ squeezers

Smooth muscle works automatically in the walls of hollow organs, such as the stomach and bladder. When it contracts, it squeezes those organs. Smooth muscle fibers in the irises of the eyes control the size of the pupils.

Smooth muscle has sheets of short fibers that wrap around hollow organs. Under a microscope, the fibers' nuclei appear as dark specks.

Inside a muscle

Each skeletal muscle has a highly ordered structure, as shown by this "exploded" view. When instructed by the brain, each fiber of a skeletal muscle contracts to give the muscle its pulling power.

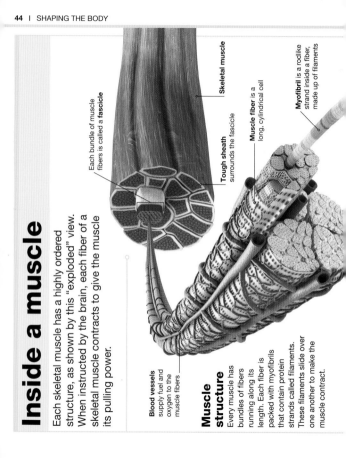

Skeletal muscle

Each bundle of muscle fibers is called a **fascicle**

Tough sheath surrounds the fascicle

Muscle fiber is a long, cylindrical cell

Myofibril is a rodlike strand inside a fiber, made up of filaments

Blood vessels supply fuel and oxygen to the muscle fibers

Muscle structure

Every muscle has bundles of fibers running along its length. Each fiber is packed with myofibrils that contain protein strands called filaments. These filaments slide over one another to make the muscle contract.

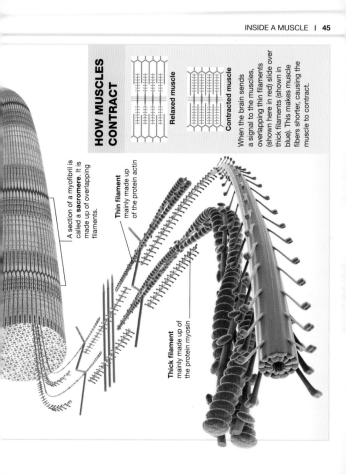

HOW MUSCLES CONTRACT

Relaxed muscle

Contracted muscle

When the brain sends a signal to the muscles, overlapping thin filaments (shown here in red) slide over thick filaments (shown in blue). This makes muscle fibers shorter, causing the muscle to contract.

A section of a myofibril is called a **sacromere**. It is made up of overlapping filaments.

Thin filament
mainly made up of the protein actin

Thick filament
mainly made up of the protein myosin

The muscles that move the eyeballs
react faster than any other body
muscle, contracting in just
$1/100$ **seconds**

SKELETAL MUSCLE
This SEM image shows a muscle fiber—one of the cells that make up skeletal muscle—that has been cut in two. It is packed with strands called filaments (shown in brown), which move to make the muscle contract.

How muscles work

When skeletal muscles get instructions from the brain, they use energy to contract (shorten) and pull bones. Once the movement is complete, they relax and lengthen. Facial muscles tug at the skin of the face to produce different expressions.

In opposition

Muscles can pull but not push, so they are arranged in pairs that have opposite actions. For example, in the upper arm the biceps and triceps muscles work in opposition to bend or straighten the arm.

Bending the elbow

Biceps contracts and pulls the forearm upward

Triceps relaxes and lengthens at the back of the arm

Finger pullers

The muscles that move the fingers are found mostly in the forearm. They are attached to the finger bones by long tendons that cross the wrist. Forearm muscles on the same side as the palm bend the fingers, while those on the same side as the back of the hand straighten the fingers.

Straightening the elbow

Triceps contracts and pulls the forearm downward

Biceps relaxes and gets longer

FACE SHAPERS

Facial expressions are created by more than 30 small muscles that pull the skin.

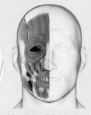

Muscles pull the corners of the mouth upward and outward and lift the top lip when a person **smiles**.

If a person is **sad**, the corners of the mouth are pulled downward and the eyebrows are wrinkled.

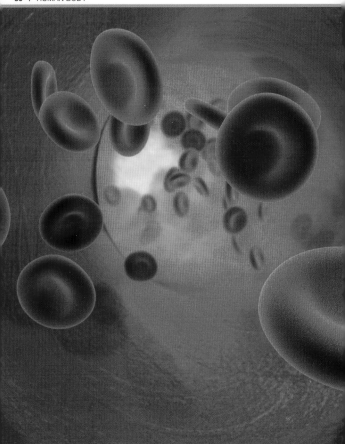

Blood and lymph

To work at their best, cells must have stable surroundings. Three body systems make this happen. The blood system delivers food and oxygen to cells, removes their waste matter, and keeps them warm. The lymph system drains surplus fluid from tissues and works with the blood system to kill germs. The urinary system removes waste from the blood and disposes of it in urine.

THE HEART
The heart beats 100,000 times each day to pump blood along a vast network of blood vessels. Stretched out, these would wrap around the world three times.

Blood system

The body's trillions of cells need a constant supply of oxygen and food, which is provided by the blood, or circulatory, system. This is made up of the heart and a network of tubes called blood vessels.

Network of vessels

Blood vessels carry blood to every part of the body, from head to toe. Arteries (shown in red) carry blood away from the heart. Veins (shown in blue) carry blood back to the heart. They are linked by tiny capillaries that are too small to be seen here.

Carotid artery supplies the head and brain with oxygen and food

Aorta, the body's biggest blood vessel, carries blood away from the heart

Pulmonary artery carries blood from the heart to the lungs

The heart pumps blood to the lungs to collect oxygen and to the body to deliver oxygen

Descending aorta carries blood toward the abdomen and legs

Inferior vena cava carries blood from the abdomen and legs to the heart

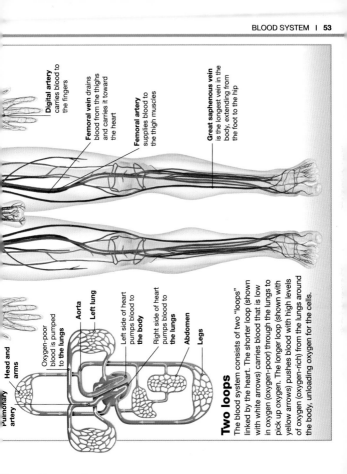

Digital artery carries blood to the fingers

Femoral vein drains blood from the thighs and carries it toward the heart

Femoral artery supplies blood to the thigh muscles

Great saphenous vein is the longest vein in the body, extending from the foot to the hip

Pulmonary artery

Head and arms

Oxygen-poor blood is pumped to **the lungs**

Aorta

Left lung

Left side of heart pumps blood to **the body**

Right side of heart pumps blood to **the lungs**

Abdomen

Legs

Two loops

The blood system consists of two "loops" linked by the heart. The shorter loop (shown with white arrows) carries blood that is low in oxygen (oxygen-poor) through the lungs to pick up oxygen. The longer loop (shown with yellow arrows) pushes blood with high levels of oxygen (oxygen-rich) from the lungs around the body, unloading oxygen for the cells.

Blood vessels

Three types of blood vessel carry blood around the body. Arteries transport blood away from the heart, veins carry blood toward the heart, and tiny capillaries carry blood through tissues and link arteries to veins. Altogether, the body's blood vessels extend over 60,000 miles (100,000 km).

Capillary network

Vast networks of capillaries weave their way through body tissues to supply cells with food and oxygen. Capillaries branch out from tiny arteries and then merge together to form tiny veins.

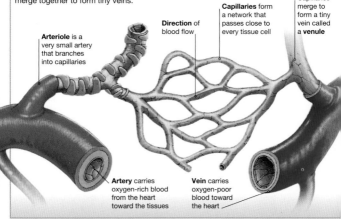

Capillaries form a network that passes close to every tissue cell

Capillaries merge to form a tiny vein called a **venule**

Direction of blood flow

Arteriole is a very small artery that branches into capillaries

Artery carries oxygen-rich blood from the heart toward the tissues

Vein carries oxygen-poor blood toward the heart

Living tubes

Arteries have thick, muscular walls to cope with the high pressure created when the heart pumps blood. Microscopic capillaries make deliveries to individual cells. Thin-walled veins carry blood under low pressure back to the heart.

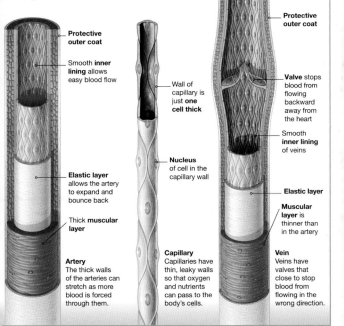

Protective outer coat

Smooth inner lining allows easy blood flow

Wall of capillary is just **one** cell thick

Protective outer coat

Valve stops blood from flowing backward away from the heart

Smooth **inner lining** of veins

Elastic layer allows the artery to expand and bounce back

Nucleus of cell in the capillary wall

Thick **muscular layer**

Elastic layer

Muscular layer is thinner than in the artery

Artery
The thick walls of the arteries can stretch as more blood is forced through them.

Capillary
Capillaries have thin, leaky walls so that oxygen and nutrients can pass to the body's cells.

Vein
Veins have valves that close to stop blood from flowing in the wrong direction.

Two million

red blood cells are made and
another two million worn-out
cells are destroyed every second

RED BLOOD CELLS
The flattened, dimpled shape of red blood cells is ideal for their role as oxygen carriers. It provides a large surface for both absorbing oxygen in the lungs and releasing oxygen in the tissues, making red blood cells incredibly efficient.

The heart

The heart is the powerhouse of the circulatory system. It beats around 70 times a minute to push blood around the body. The heart is made of cardiac muscle, which never tires.

Superior vena cava carries blood into the right atrium

Inside the heart

The heart has a left and a right side, each with two chambers—the atrium and the ventricle. The right side of the heart pumps blood to the lungs, while the left side pumps blood to the body. Valves stop the blood from flowing in the wrong direction.

Right atrium

Valve between the atrium and ventricle

Heart strings are thin cords attached to the valve between each atrium and ventricle. When the heart beats, these strings stop the valve from turning inside out like an umbrella in a strong wind.

Right ventricle

Inferior vena cava carries blood from the lower body

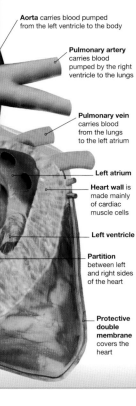

Aorta carries blood pumped from the left ventricle to the body

Pulmonary artery carries blood pumped by the right ventricle to the lungs

Pulmonary vein carries blood from the lungs to the left atrium

Left atrium

Heart wall is made mainly of cardiac muscle cells

Left ventricle

Partition between left and right sides of the heart

Protective double membrane covers the heart

Feeding the heart

Cardiac muscle cells in the wall of the heart need a constant supply of food and oxygen to give them the energy to contract and keep the heart beating. Deliveries are made to cardiac muscle cells through a network of arteries, called coronary arteries, that run through the wall of the heart.

Specialized X-ray of the heart, showing arteries in red

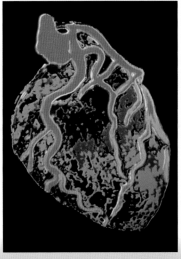

Heartbeat

The fist-sized heart is an amazing double pump. Its right and left sides beat together to push blood to the lungs and body. In an average lifetime, the heart beats around 2.5 billion times without taking a break.

Beating heart

Every heartbeat is made up of three stages. In the first stage, blood is drawn into the atria—the heart's upper chambers. In the second, blood is pushed into the ventricles below. In the final stage, blood is pushed out of the heart. Valves in the heart keep the blood flowing in one direction.

A baby's heart beats for the first time during the fourth week of pregnancy, when the baby is the size of a fingernail.

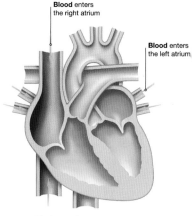

Blood enters the right atrium

Blood enters the left atrium

The **heart relaxes** and oxygen-poor blood flows into the right atrium, while oxygen-rich blood flows into the left atrium.

Hearing heartbeats

A doctor uses a stethoscope to listen to a person's heart and check if the heart valves are working properly. When the valves between the atria and the ventricles close, they make a loud "lub" sound, and when the semilunar valves slam shut, they make a shorter, sharper "dup" sound.

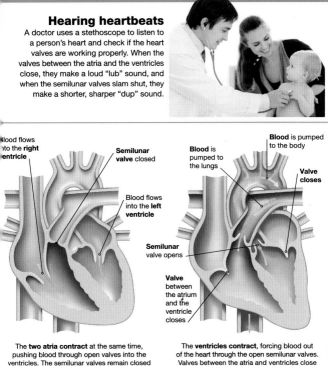

Blood flows into the **right ventricle**

Semilunar valve closed

Blood flows into the **left ventricle**

Blood is pumped to the lungs

Blood is pumped to the body

Valve closes

Semilunar valve opens

Valve between the atrium and the ventricle closes

The **two atria contract** at the same time, pushing blood through open valves into the ventricles. The semilunar valves remain closed to stop blood from flowing backward.

The **ventricles contract**, forcing blood out of the heart through the open semilunar valves. Valves between the atria and ventricles close to prevent backflow.

What's in blood?

Blood is made up of trillions of cells floating in plasma (a watery liquid). Pumped by the heart, blood supplies the body with food, oxygen, and other essentials. Blood also carries heat around the body and helps to protect it against germs.

Types of blood cell

There are three main types of blood cell. Red blood cells, which make up one-quarter of the body's cells, transport oxygen from the lungs to the tissues. White blood cells kill disease-causing germs. Platelets help in creating blood clots to plug leaks.

Red blood cell

White blood cell

BLOOD COMPONENTS

Red blood cells are filled with hemoglobin, a protein that is able to pick up and release oxygen. These cells also give blood its red color.

White blood cells and platelets aid the body's defenses. White blood cells detect and destroy invading germs, while platelets help to heal wounds.

Plasma is 90 percent water. The remaining 10 percent is made up of about 100 dissolved substances including nutrients, waste matter, and hormones.

Platelet

**Wall of the
blood vessel**

Plasma is a straw-colored liquid that makes up **55 percent** of blood

White blood cells and platelets make up **1 percent** of blood

Red blood cells make up the remaining **44 percent** of blood

In the mix

Plasma makes up the greatest part of blood, followed by red blood cells and then white blood cells and platelets. A single pinhead-sized drop of blood contains about 2.5 million red blood cells, 3,750 white blood cells, and 160,000 platelets.

Blood clotting

Damage to a blood vessel automatically triggers a chain of events to repair the wound. The blood becomes sticky to block the leak and prevent harmful germs from entering the body. Then the blood clots to seal the wound and allow the damage to be repaired.

Healing the wound

When an injury happens, such as a cut to the skin, the damage could be dangerous. To stop the loss of blood and avoid infection, all three types of blood cell take action.

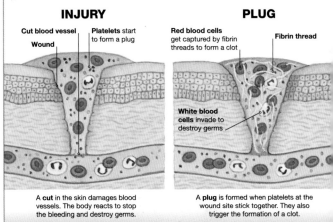

INJURY

Cut blood vessel
Wound
Platelets start to form a plug

PLUG

Red blood cells get captured by fibrin threads to form a clot
Fibrin thread
White blood cells invade to destroy germs

A **cut** in the skin damages blood vessels. The body reacts to stop the bleeding and destroy germs.

A **plug** is formed when platelets at the wound site stick together. They also trigger the formation of a clot.

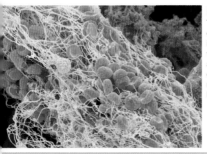

Fibrin threads

Taken using a scanning electron microscope, this image shows a magnified view of a blood clot shortly after it formed. The red blood cells are trapped in a tight mesh of fibrin threads that looks like a fishing net.

CLOT

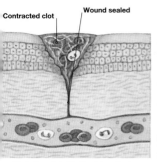

Contracted clot

Wound sealed

Fibrin threads inside the clot contract and pull the edges of the wound together to prevent leakage.

SCAB

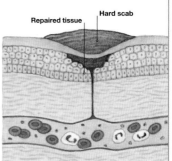

Repaired tissue

Hard scab

A **scab** is formed on the surface of the clot. The hard scab protects the wound site as tissues are repaired.

Fighting disease

The body is constantly under threat from microscopic, disease-causing organisms such as bacteria and viruses (known more commonly as germs). Outer barriers, such as the skin, and an internal immune system stop germs from getting into and multiplying inside the body.

Body barriers

The body has a number of physical defenses to stop infection. Cells lining hollow organs are packed together tightly to stop germs from reaching the tissues beneath them. Special protective fluids, such as mucus, saliva, and gastric juice, help to trap and kill germs.

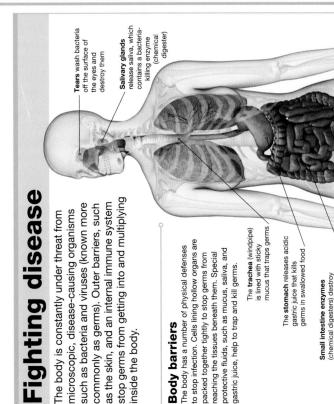

Tears wash bacteria off the surface of the eyes and destroy them

Salivary glands release saliva, which contains a bacteria-killing enzyme (chemical digester)

The **trachea** (windpipe) is lined with sticky mucus that traps germs

The **stomach** releases acidic gastric juice that kills germs in swallowed food

Small intestine enzymes (chemical digesters) destroy

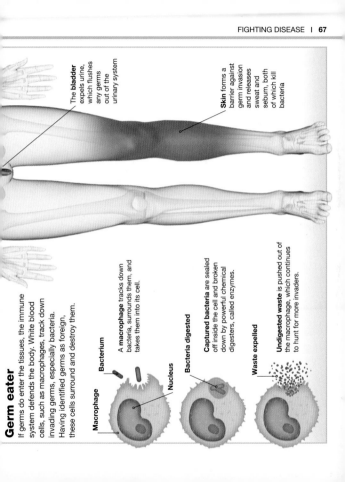

The **bladder** expels urine, which flushes any germs out of the urinary system

Skin forms a barrier against germ invasion and releases sweat and sebum, both of which kill bacteria

Germ eater

If germs do enter the tissues, the immune system defends the body. White blood cells, such as macrophages, track down invading germs, especially bacteria. Having identified germs as foreign, these cells surround and destroy them.

Macrophage

Bacterium

A **macrophage** tracks down bacteria, surrounds them, and takes them into its cell.

Nucleus

Bacteria digested

Captured **bacteria** are sealed off inside the cell and broken down by powerful chemical digesters, called enzymes.

Waste expelled

Undigested **waste** is pushed out of the macrophage, which continues to hunt for more invaders.

Laughing
every day makes the immune system more efficient at defending the body

GERM KILLER
The word "macrophage" means "big eater." This germ-killing macrophage (shown in blue) has tracked down invading bacteria (shown in green) and is stretching out to capture them. It will then digest the bacteria and display markers that identify the bacteria for other defense cells.

The body's drain

As blood circulates through tissues it leaves behind fluid. The fluid is known as lymph when it drains from the tissue into the lymphatic system. This one-way system of vessels returns lymph to the circulatory system. Along the way, lymph is also filtered to remove germs.

Lymphatic system

Lymph vessels (shown in purple) extend to all parts of the body. Tiny lymph capillaries drain fluid from tissues and then merge to form larger lymph vessels. Two main tubes, or ducts, in the chest empty into the bloodstream. The system also contains swellings called lymph nodes and several organs, such as the tonsils and spleen. These contain immune system cells that kill germs.

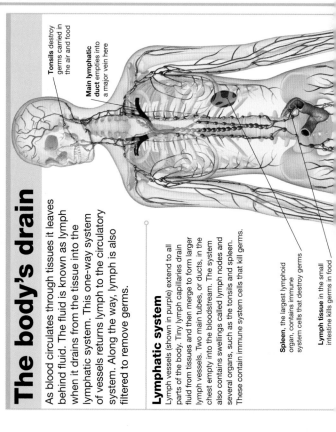

Tonsils destroy germs carried in the air and food

Main lymphatic duct empties into a major vein here

Spleen, the largest lymphoid organ, contains immune system cells that destroy germs

Lymph tissue in the small intestine kills germs in food

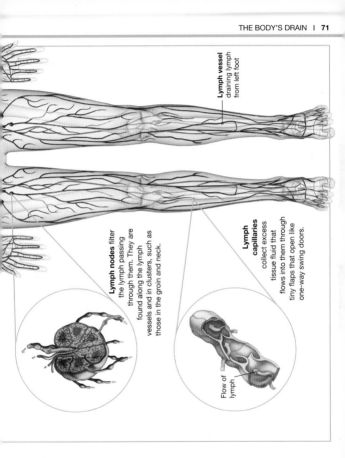

Lymph vessel draining lymph from left foot

Lymph nodes filter the lymph passing through them. They are found along the lymph vessels and in clusters, such as those in the groin and neck.

Lymph capillaries collect excess tissue fluid that flows into them through tiny flaps that open like one-way swing doors.

Flow of lymph

Filtering blood

The kidneys and other parts of the urinary system play a key part in controlling what is in the blood. The kidneys filter blood to remove poisonous substances as well as excess water and salt to make urine. The cleaned blood then flows back into the bloodstream.

Urinary system

The urinary system is made up of two kidneys, two ureters, a bladder, and a urethra. The kidneys produce urine, which is pushed down the ureters to the bladder. It is stored here before being released from the body through the urethra.

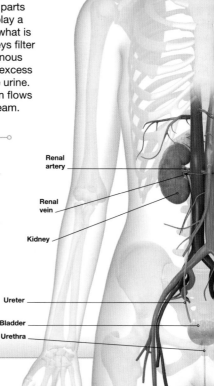

Renal artery

Renal vein

Kidney

Ureter

Bladder

Urethra

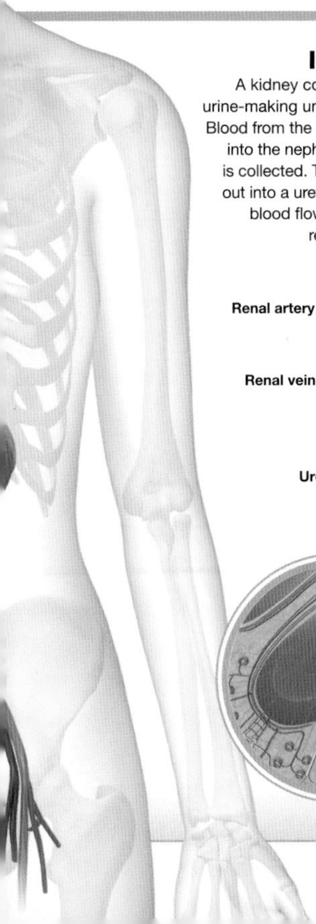

Inside a kidney

A kidney contains about a million urine-making units called nephrons. Blood from the renal artery passes into the nephrons, where urine is collected. The urine empties out into a ureter and the clean blood flows back into the rest of the body.

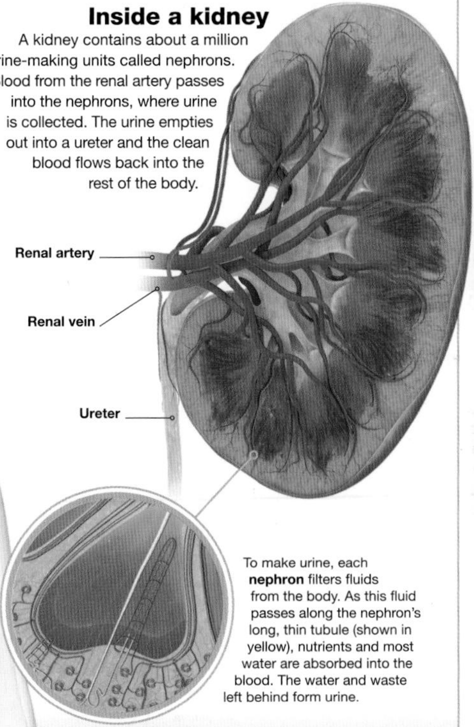

Renal artery

Renal vein

Ureter

To make urine, each **nephron** filters fluids from the body. As this fluid passes along the nephron's long, thin tubule (shown in yellow), nutrients and most water are absorbed into the blood. The water and waste left behind form urine.

Getting rid of waste

The kidneys release a constant dribble of urine at all times of the day. This urine passes into a stretchy muscular bag—the bladder—where it is stored until we feel the need to release it. Water lost from the body in urine is replaced by the water in food and drink.

Filling and emptying

The bladder's exit is normally closed by two rings of muscle called sphincters. As the bladder fills up, a person will feel the need to urinate (go to the bathroom). The sphincters relax and urine is squeezed out by the bladder's muscular wall.

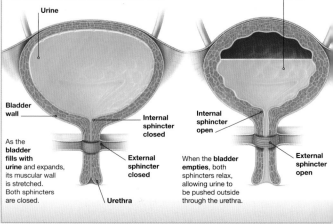

Urine

Bladder wall

Internal sphincter closed

As the **bladder fills with urine** and expands, its muscular wall is stretched. Both sphincters are closed.

External sphincter closed

Urethra

Urine

Internal sphincter open

External sphincter open

When the **bladder empties**, both sphincters relax, allowing urine to be pushed outside through the urethra.

What's in urine?

About 94 percent of urine is water. The rest is dissolved substances that the body does not need. These include urea, the waste product made in the liver, and excess salt.

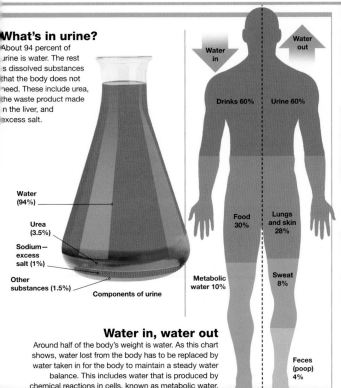

Water (94%)

Urea (3.5%)

Sodium— excess salt (1%)

Other substances (1.5%)

Components of urine

Water in

Water out

Drinks 60%

Urine 60%

Food 30%

Lungs and skin 28%

Metabolic water 10%

Sweat 8%

Feces (poop) 4%

Water in, water out

Around half of the body's weight is water. As this chart shows, water lost from the body has to be replaced by water taken in for the body to maintain a steady water balance. This includes water that is produced by chemical reactions in cells, known as metabolic water.

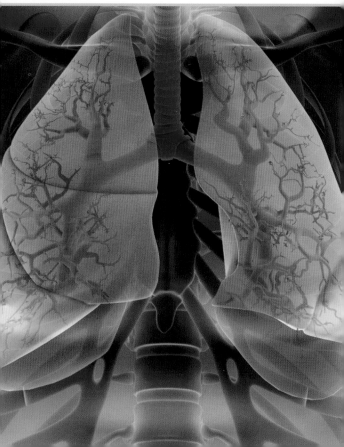

Lungs and breathing

The human body cannot survive without a nonstop supply of oxygen from the air. The trillions of body cells need constant deliveries of oxygen to release the energy that powers their activities. This process also generates the waste gas carbon dioxide. To get oxygen into the body and to remove carbon dioxide, air is breathed into and out of the lungs.

MISTY BREATH
The air we breathe out, or exhale, contains droplets of water from the lungs. On cold days, these water droplets show up as a fine mist in the air.

Breathing system

Also called the respiratory system, the breathing system is made up of two lungs and the tubes, or airways, that carry air into and out of the body. Inside the lungs, those airways divide over and over again to form smaller and smaller branches.

The **nasal cavity** is a space behind the nose where the air we breathe is cleaned. Mucus traps dirt and germs and tiny hairlike cilia sweep the mucus to the throat.

Branching airways

Air travels through the nasal cavity and along the windpipe, or trachea. At its base, the trachea splits into two smaller tubes, called bronchi (each one is called a bronchus), which go into the lungs. These go into narrower and narrower bronchi and bronchioles.

The **right lung** is larger than the left, which has to make room for the heart

Alveoli are tiny air bags found at the ends of the bronchioles. Oxygen passes into the bloodstream through the walls of the alveoli.

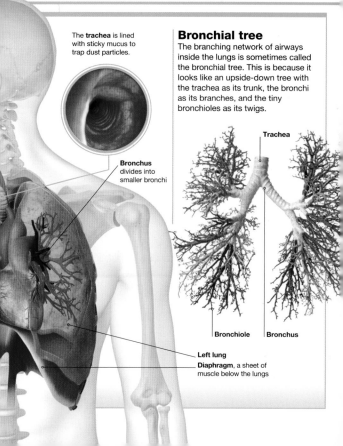

The **trachea** is lined with sticky mucus to trap dust particles.

Bronchus divides into smaller bronchi

Bronchial tree

The branching network of airways inside the lungs is sometimes called the bronchial tree. This is because it looks like an upside-down tree with the trachea as its trunk, the bronchi as its branches, and the tiny bronchioles as its twigs.

Trachea

Bronchiole

Bronchus

Left lung

Diaphragm, a sheet of muscle below the lungs

Breathe in, breathe out

Breathing in and out brings oxygen into the lungs and removes the harmful waste gas, carbon dioxide. The process involves the diaphragm and the intercostal muscles, which are found between the ribs.

Intercostal muscles pull the ribs upward and outward

Lungs expand as the chest gets bigger

Diaphragm contracts, flattens, and pushes downward

Air in...

The diaphragm and intercostal muscles contract (tighten) to increase the size of the space inside the chest. As this happens, the lungs expand and fresh air enters from outside.

ir passes
ut through
e nose
nd mouth

ungs shrink
s the chest
ets smaller

IN CONTROL

The rate of breathing
is controlled automatically
by the brain stem at the
base of the brain. During
exercise, such as running,
the breathing rate increases
to get extra oxygen to the
hard-working muscles.

Diaphragm relaxes
and is pushed upward
into a dome shape by
organs below

... Air out

The diaphragm and
intercostal muscles
relax so that the ribs
move downward
and inward. This
squeezes the lungs,
pushing air out of
the body.

Inside the lungs

The lungs contain around 300 million microscopic alveoli at the ends of the airways. Oxygen enters the blood and carbon dioxide is removed through these tiny air bags.

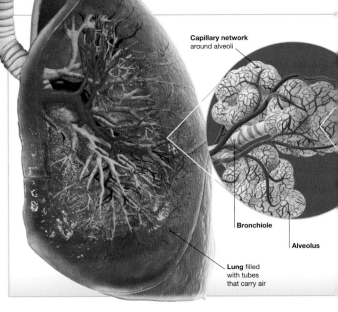

Capillary network
around alveoli

Bronchiole

Alveolus

Lung filled
with tubes
that carry air

Exchanging gases

Blood flowing through the capillaries (tiny blood vessels) surrounding the alveoli constantly picks up oxygen and carries it to the body's cells. At the same time, it dumps carbon dioxide into the alveoli to be breathed out.

Capillary wall lets oxygen pass into the red blood cells and carbon dioxide into the alveolus

Carbon dioxide out

Oxygen in

Inside of alveolus

Oxygen travels into the blood

Blood flowing around an alveolus changes from being low in oxygen (blue) to being rich in oxygen (red)

Carbon dioxide travels into the alveolus

Speech

People can communicate with each other using speech. The sounds we speak are produced by special breathing movements. These send bursts of air through the sound-creating vocal cords found in the throat.

Making sounds

During normal breathing the vocal cords are pulled open to allow air to be breathed in and out. While we are speaking, muscles pull the vocal cords together. When air is pushed between the closed vocal cords, they vibrate and produce sounds.

The **larynx**, or voice box, links the throat to the trachea, or windpipe, and contains the vocal cords. It is made from pieces of cartilage.

Vocal cords stretch from the front to the back of the larynx

Rings of cartilage hold the trachea open

Vocal cords pulled closed

Trachea carries air to and from the lungs

Shaping words

Vibrations of the vocal cords produce humming sounds. Muscles move the tongue, lips, and cheeks to shape these sounds into the words we want to say.

Open mouth forms an "ah" sound

Pursed open lips form an "oo" sound

Pharynx (throat)

The **epiglottis** is a flap that covers the larynx during swallowing, to stop food from getting into the trachea

Vocal cords pulled open

Esophagus

About 6,900 languages are spoken across the world. The most common are Mandarin Chinese, English, Spanish, Hindi, and Russian.

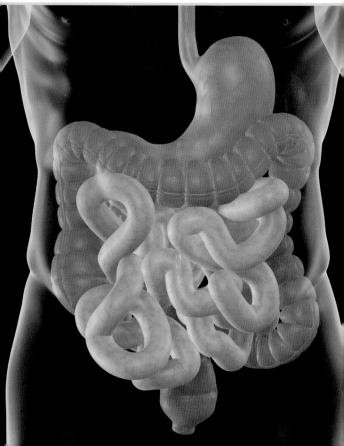

The digestive system

An average person eats about 20 tons of food in a lifetime. The digestive system transforms this mountain of meals into substances that the body can use. The system breaks food down into simple nutrients that supply energy to body cells and provide the chemicals needed to make the body grow, maintain, and repair itself.

FRIENDLY BACTERIA
Inside the intestines are trillions of "friendly" bacteria, such as *Lactobacillus fermentum*. They release extra nutrients from food for the body to use.

Feeding the body

Before we can use the food we eat, it must be broken down, or digested, into simple nutrients. These nutrients are then absorbed into the bloodstream and carried to the body's cells.

Digestive system

The digestive tract is a tube that runs from the mouth to the anus. Each part of the tract plays its own part in digestion. Other organs, such as the teeth, salivary glands, and liver, also help with digestion.

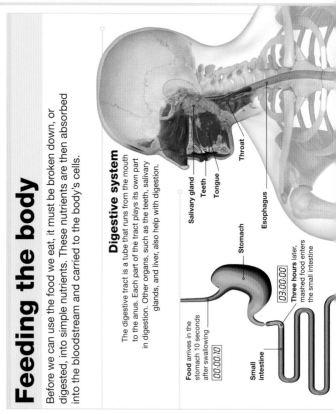

Salivary gland

Teeth

Tongue

Throat

Esophagus

Stomach

Three hours later, mashed food enters the small intestine
03:00:00

Food arrives in the stomach 10 seconds after swallowing
00:00:10

Small intestine

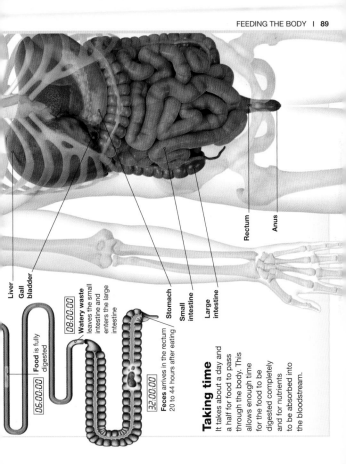

Liver

Gall
bladder

Rectum

Anus

05:00:00 **Food** is fully
digested

08:00:00 **Watery waste**
leaves the small
intestine and
enters the large
intestine

Stomach

Small
intestine

Large
intestine

32:00:00 **Feces** arrives in the rectum
20 to 44 hours after eating

Taking time

It takes about a day and
a half for food to pass
through the body. This
allows enough time
for the food to be
digested completely
and for nutrients
to be absorbed into
the bloodstream.

Chew and swallow

The mouth is the first part of the digestive tract. Here, chunks of food are chewed and crushed by the teeth into pieces small enough to be pushed into the throat by the tongue, and swallowed.

Mouth and throat

The mouth contains the teeth and tongue. During chewing, the tongue mixes the food with slimy saliva released by salivary glands. The resulting slippery ball of food is then swallowed.

Food

Teeth

The tongue moves and mixes food

Salivary glands release saliva

Throat

The **epiglottis** blocks entrance to trachea (windpipe) during swallowing

The **esophagus** carries food to the stomach

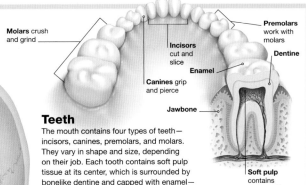

Molars crush and grind

Premolars work with molars

Incisors cut and slice

Dentine

Enamel

Canines grip and pierce

Jawbone

Soft pulp contains nerve endings

Teeth

The mouth contains four types of teeth—incisors, canines, premolars, and molars. They vary in shape and size, depending on their job. Each tooth contains soft pulp tissue at its center, which is surrounded by bonelike dentine and capped with enamel—the body's hardest substance.

SWALLOWING

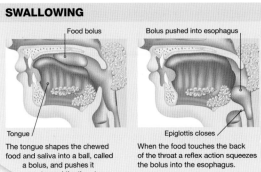

Food bolus

Bolus pushed into esophagus

Tongue

Epiglottis closes

The tongue shapes the chewed food and saliva into a ball, called a bolus, and pushes it toward the throat.

When the food touches the back of the throat a reflex action squeezes the bolus into the esophagus.

Into the stomach

The stomach mixes chewed food with gastric juice, a liquid that contains an enzyme (chemical digester) that breaks down proteins. The stomach also stores food, releasing it slowly so that the small intestine has time to digest it.

The **esophagus** delivers food from the mouth

Muscular bag

The baglike stomach has a stretchy wall so that it can expand during a meal. The wall has three layers of muscles that contract to squash and squeeze the food, churning it up and mixing it with the gastric juice.

The **duodenum** is the first part of the small intestine

Folds in the stomach lining disappear as it fills with food

The **pyloric sphincter** is a ring of muscle that remains tightly closed when the stomach processes food.

Chyme is a mixture of part-digested food and gastric juice

Three muscle layers run around and along the stomach

Gastric glands in the stomach wall release gastric juice into the stomach through openings called gastric pits.

Filling and emptying

The process of filling and emptying the stomach takes at least three hours. During this time, the food is partially digested and churned into a creamy liquid called chyme. The semidigested, liquid food is then released into the duodenum through the open pyloric sphincter.

During a meal, **food** is mixed with gastric juice

About 1–2 hours after eating, the **pyloric sphincter** is closed to keep food in the stomach

Stomach wall contracts to churn food into chyme

Around 3–4 hours after eating, **chyme** is pushed through the open pyloric sphincter

Small intestine

With help from the gall bladder and pancreas, the small intestine completes digestion, using enzymes. These chemical digesters break down the proteins, carbohydrates, and fats in foods into simple nutrients that are absorbed into the bloodstream.

The **large intestine** lies in front of the duodenum

Small intestine

The small intestine is nearly 23 ft (7 m) long and has three sections. The shortest is the duodenum. The middle jejunum and final ileum are where most digestion and absorption take place.

Jejunum

Extra help

Two liquids kick-start digestion in the small intestine. Bile turns fats into tiny droplets that are easier to break down. Pancreatic juice contains enzymes that digest proteins and carbohydrates.

Ileum

The **gall bladder** stores bile made in the liver

Bile duct carries bile toward the duodenum

Pancreatic duct carries pancreatic juice toward the duodenum

Opening of bile and pancreatic ducts into the duodenum

Pancreas makes pancreatic juice

Lining the wall of the small intestine are millions of fingerlike **villi**. These provide a huge surface area for absorbing nutrients.

Villi

Muscular wall

Peristalsis

Muscles contract and relax in waves to push food along the small intestine and other parts of the digestive tract. This is called peristalsis.

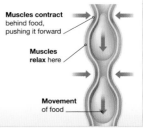

Muscles contract behind food, pushing it forward

Muscles relax here

Movement of food

VILLI
The inside of the small intestine is lined with tiny fingerlike projections called villi, which are about 0.04 in (1 mm) long. Together they cover an area of 2,800 sq ft (260 sq m). Villi give the inside of the intestine a velvety texture, just like a soft towel. They transfer nutrients into the bloodstream.

pread out, the lining of the inside
f the small intestine would cover a

ennis court

Large intestine

The large intestine is about a quarter of the length of the small intestine, but twice its width. It receives watery waste from the small intestine and turns it into semisolid feces (poop).

Three parts

The cecum, colon, and rectum make up the large intestine. The longest section, the colon, travels up, across, and down the abdomen. It turns watery, undigested waste into feces by absorbing water back into the bloodstream.

Transverse colon travels across the abdomen

Ascending colon rises up the abdomen

Descending colon passes down the abdomen

The **cecum** is the first, short section of the large intestine

Junction between small and large intestines

Feces

The **appendix** sticks out from the cecum

Rectum stores feces ready for disposal

Anus opens for feces to leave the body

Each day, the average person passes enough wind (gas from the large intestine) to fill a party balloon.

Colon movements

Three types of muscular movement push waste along the colon as is turned into feces. These slow movements are made by smooth muscles that run along and around the walls of the large intestine.

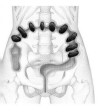

Segmentation movements are produced by a series of short contractions all along the colon that mix and churn feces but do not move them.

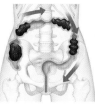

Peristalsis movements involve small contractions that pass along the colon in waves and push feces toward the rectum.

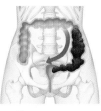

Mass movements are extra-strong contractions that happen three or four times a day after eating and push feces into the rectum.

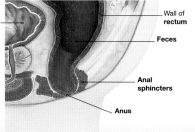

Bladder stores urine

Wall of **rectum**

Feces

Anal sphincters

Anus

Pushed outside

As feces is pushed into the rectum, it stretches the rectum wall. This triggers the need to go to the bathroom. The anal sphincter muscles relax, and the rectum wall contracts to push the feces out through the anus.

The liver

The liver is the body's largest internal organ, and all of our blood flows through it. The liver cells remove and add substances to help clean the blood. This helps to keep conditions stable inside the body.

Liver

The **gall bladder** stores bile

Liver cells perform over 500 functions, including storing nutrients and removing poisons from blood. They also make bile, which is used to help digest fats.

Large intestine

The **small intestine** is where most nutrients are absorbed into the bloodstream

Blood supply

The liver receives 80 percent of its blood from the hepatic portal vein. Veins carry the blood from the digestive organs to the hepatic portal vein, which then enters the liver. This blood is rich in nutrients, which the liver processes in its cells.

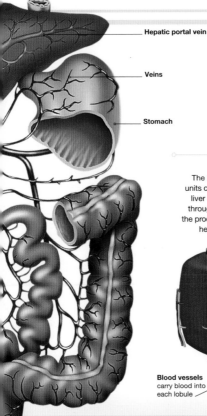

Hepatic portal vein

Veins

Stomach

The liver stores glucose—the body's fuel—when there's too much of it in the blood and releases it when there is too little.

Inside the liver

The liver contains a million processing units called lobules. Inside these lobules, liver cells process the blood that flows through the liver. A central vein collects the processed blood to be returned to the heart and pumped around the body.

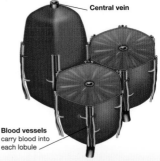

Central vein

Blood vessels
carry blood into each lobule

Controlling the body

Running throughout the body is a network called the nervous system, which is made up of long, thin nerve cells. This network carries tiny electrical signals from sensors all around the body to the body's control center—the brain. These signals tell the brain what is happening in the world around it and carry messages from the brain to the body, telling it to perform a range of activities, from breathing to balancing on tiptoe.

TOUCH
Our fingertips are very sensitive. Sensors in the skin send signals to the brain, allowing us to feel even the lightest touch.

Nervous system

Everything we do is controlled by the nervous system. This is made up of billions of neurons—interconnected cells that carry high-speed electrical signals.

Control network

Most neurons are packed into the brain and the spinal cord. Together, these make up the central nervous system and control the body's activities, communicating with the rest of the body through nerves.

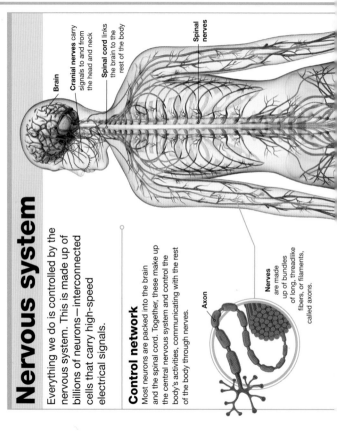

Brain

Cranial nerves carry signals to and from the head and neck

Spinal cord links the brain to the rest of the body

Spinal nerves

Nerves are made up of bundles of long, threadlike fibers, or filaments, called axons.

Axon

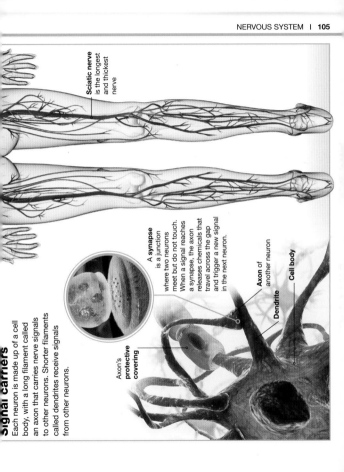

Sciatic nerve is the longest and thickest nerve

Signal carriers

Each neuron is made up of a cell body, with a long filament called an axon that carries nerve signals to other neurons. Shorter filaments called dendrites receive signals from other neurons.

A synapse is a junction where two neurons meet but do not touch. When a signal reaches a synapse, the axon releases chemicals that travel across the gap and trigger a new signal in the next neuron.

Axon's **protective covering**

Axon of another neuron

Dendrite

Cell body

The brain

The 100 billion neurons in the brain form a control network of incredible power. The brain gives us our personality and allows us to think, remember, and sense our surroundings. It also coordinates almost all bodily activities, from running to digestion.

Inside the brain

This cross-section through the brain shows its three parts. The cerebrum lets us think, feel, and move. The cerebellum organizes movement and balance. The brain stem controls vital functions such as our heartbeat and breathing rate.

Premotor cortex **organizes complex movements**

Prefrontal cortex is the area involved with **thinking and personality**

The **cerebrum** is the largest part of the brain

Cerebellum

Brain stem

Spinal cord

Broca's area **controls speech**

Auditory association cortex **identifies sounds**

Motor cortex **sends signals to the muscles**

Sensory cortex **receives information about touch**

Brain map

The thin outer layer of the cerebrum is called the cerebral cortex. Packed with neurons, it receives and processes incoming signals and sends out instructions. Different areas of the cerebral cortex are responsible for specific jobs.

Sensory association cortex **identifies skin sensations**

Visual association cortex **turns visual signals into images**

Wernicke's area **understands words**

Primary visual cortex **receives signals from the eyes**

Primary auditory cortex **interprets signals from the ears**

Cerebellum

The fastest neurons can transmit nerve signals at up to

220 mph

(350 kph)

BRAIN CELLS
This microscopic view of brain neurons—nerve cells—shows the links between them. Each neuron makes up to 10,000 connections with other neurons, creating a network that allows the brain to process millions of pieces of information at the same time.

Spinal cord

The spinal cord carries the signals that help control the body. It is a bundle of billions of neurons that stretches down the back from the brain. About the width of a finger, it connects the brain to the rest of the body.

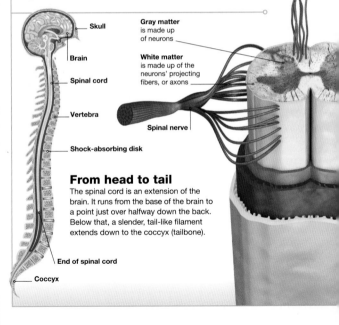

Skull

Brain

Spinal cord

Vertebra

Shock-absorbing disk

Gray matter is made up of neurons

White matter is made up of the neurons' projecting fibers, or axons

Spinal nerve

From head to tail

The spinal cord is an extension of the brain. It runs from the base of the brain to a point just over halfway down the back. Below that, a slender, tail-like filament extends down to the coccyx (tailbone).

End of spinal cord

Coccyx

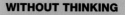

rotating the spinal cord

e bundle of neurons that forms the spinal cord
made of soft tissue. This is protected
a tunnel of bone formed by
e vertebrae that make
the backbone.
ese vertebrae
separated
thick disks
cartilage.

Information highway

A cross-section through the spinal cord
shows butterfly-shaped gray matter in
the center. The gray matter transmits
signals across the cord. These signals
are received from, and passed to, spinal
nerves, which provide the link to the
rest of the body. The white matter
relays signals to and from the brain.

WITHOUT THINKING

Reflexes are automatic actions that
happen without our being aware of
them. Many reflexes, such as this
withdrawal reflex, protect the body
from danger and are controlled by the
spinal cord. Reflex actions happen
quickly because nerve signals travel
through the spinal cord without going
to the brain.

Danger
Pain receptors
detect the burning
heat of the flame
and send signals
to the spinal cord.

Withdrawal
The spinal cord
sends signals to
an arm muscle that
pulls the hand away
from the candle.

Pain
A message is now
sent up the spinal
cord to the brain and
the person feels pain.

Seeing

Our most important sense, sight, depends on our two eyes detecting light from our surroundings. Like a digital camera, each eye automatically adjusts its focus to give us clear, sharp images.

The **retina** contains light detectors called rods (white) and cones (green). Cones detect color and detail and work best in strong light, while rods work best in dim light.

Optic nerve carries signals to the brain

Inside the eye

Light enters the eye through the cornea and then passes through the pupil and the lens. The cornea and lens focus the light to form a sharp image on the retina at the back of the eyeball. When hit by light, the retina sends signals along the optic nerve to the brain.

Muscle that moves the eyeball

Pupil size

In bright light, pupils narrow to stop too much light from entering the eyes and dazzling us. In dim light, they widen to let in extra light so that we can see.

Narrow pupil

Wide pupil

Optic nerve carries a signal when light hits the retina

Right visual field is the view seen by the left half of each retina

Right visual cortex

Left visual cortex

Left visual field is the view seen by the right half of each retina

The **thalamus** relays signals from eyes to the visual cortex

Cornea is the clear front of the eyeball

Iris controls the size of the pupil

Pupil is a hole that allows light in

Lens helps to focus light on the retina

Brain connection

Signals from the eye are turned into images that we can "see" by the visual cortex at the back of the brain. Each eye sees a slightly different view, called a visual field. By comparing these, the brain can judge distances and create 3-D images of the world around us.

IRIS
People often have the same eye color but the patterns created by the fibers in the iris are unique to every person and can be used to identify them. This image shows a magnified view of a blue iris surrounding the pupil.

The human eye can
distinguish up to
10 million
different colors

Tasting

Being able to taste food increases our enjoyment of eating. It also warns us not to eat food that may be harmful. Sensors in the tongue can detect five tastes—sweet, sour, salty, bitter, and umami (savory).

Tongue and taste buds

When food enters the mouth, the muscular tongue moves the food around and mixes it with saliva. At the same time, 10,000 taste buds in the tongue's upper surface detect the tastes in the food and send that information to the brain.

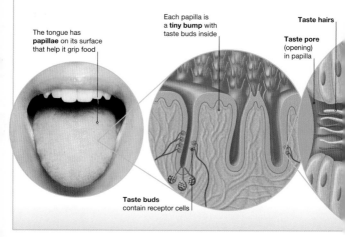

Each papilla is a **tiny bump** with taste buds inside

Taste hairs

Taste pore (opening) in papilla

The tongue has **papillae** on its surface that help it grip food

Taste buds contain receptor cells

Enjoying Flavors

Our senses of taste and smell work together and allow us to enjoy flavors. The pleasure we get from different flavors encourages us to eat and provide fuel for the body.

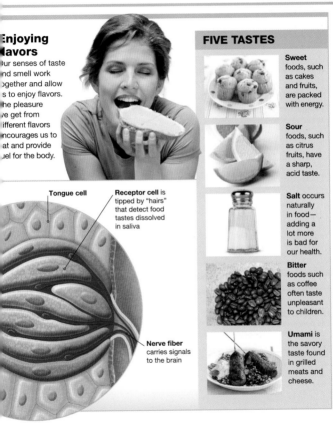

Tongue cell

Receptor cell is tipped by "hairs" that detect food tastes dissolved in saliva

Nerve fiber carries signals to the brain

FIVE TASTES

Sweet foods, such as cakes and fruits, are packed with energy.

Sour foods, such as citrus fruits, have a sharp, acid taste.

Salt occurs naturally in food—adding a lot more is bad for our health.

Bitter foods such as coffee often taste unpleasant to children.

Umami is the savory taste found in grilled meats and cheese.

Smelling

The nose has tiny detectors that pick up a vast range of smells, from freshly baked bread to the stink of rotten eggs. The smell detectors in the nose work closely with the tongue's taste sensors to allow us to appreciate flavors, too.

The **olfactory bulb** carries signals to the brain

In the roof of the nasal cavity, **odor receptor cells** detect smell molecules dissolved in watery mucus. Nerve fibers carry signals from the receptors to the olfactory bulb at the front of the brain. From there, the signals are sent to the brain.

Olfactory bulb

Nerve fiber

Skull bone

Receptor cell

Smell molecules

Air flow

Detecting smells

Air breathed in through the nose carries smell molecules. These are detected by odor receptors located at the top of the nasal cavity—the space that links the nostrils to the throat. The receptors send signals to the brain, which identifies each smell.

The **nasal cavity** channels inhaled air

The **tongue** houses taste receptors

Nerves carry signals from taste receptors to the brain

The nose contains 1,000 types of odor receptor that can detect 20,000 different smells.

Unpleasant smells

Some unpleasant smells warn us of danger. The smell of smoke might mean a building is on fire. Food that smells odd may be rotten or poisonous. When milk smells sour, it is a sign that it is not safe to drink.

Touching

The skin contains touch sensors that allow us to experience the softness of an animal's fur, the iciness of a cold swim, and much more. These skin sensors send signals to the brain, which gives us a "touch picture" of our surroundings.

Skin receptors

This cross-section through the skin shows the different types of touch sensor. Most are found in the dermis, the skin's lower layer. The nerve endings that detect heat, cold, and pain may extend into the epidermis, the skin's outer layer.

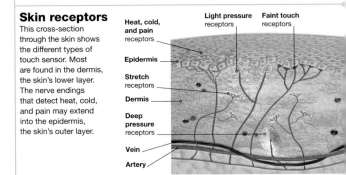

Heat, cold, and pain receptors

Light pressure receptors

Faint touch receptors

Epidermis

Stretch receptors

Dermis

Deep pressure receptors

Vein

Artery

TYPES OF TOUCH

These images show the different types of touch sensation that are detected by the skin. There is also a sixth type—pain.

Cold and heat

Light pressure

How sensitive?

Some parts of the skin are more touch-sensitive than others. This model is called a sensory homunculus (Latin for "little man") and it exaggerates the sensitive parts of the body. The more sensitive the body part, the larger it is. That is why the fingers and lips look so huge.

Sensory homunculus

Reading by touch

Our fingertips are so sensitive that they can pick up the slightest differences in the feel of an object. A visually impaired person can use touch to read, by feeling the patterns of writing printed in braille, where each letter is represented by raised dots.

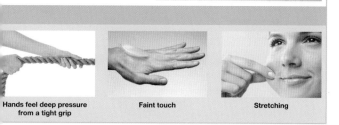

Hands feel deep pressure from a tight grip

Faint touch

Stretching

Hearing

Our ears detect sound waves that pass through the air. The sense of hearing allows us to recognize a vast range of sounds and to communicate using speech.

Skull bone

Inside the ear

The ear has three parts. The outer ear collects sound waves. In the middle ear, the sound travels as vibrations along tiny bones called ossicles. The inner ear contains a coiled cochlea that detects the vibrations and sends signals to the brain.

Ear flap directs sound into the ear canal

Cartilage provides support to the ear flap

Ear lobe is filled with fatty tissue

Outer ear canal carries sound waves toward the eardrum

Outer ear

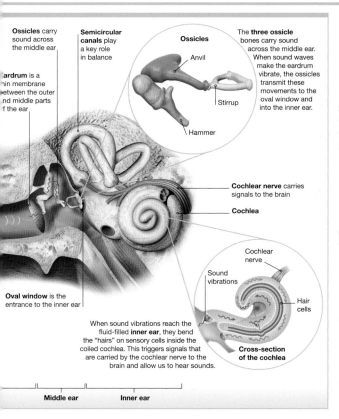

Ossicles carry sound across the middle ear

Semicircular canals play a key role in balance

Ossicles

Anvil

Stirrup

Hammer

The **three ossicle** bones carry sound across the middle ear. When sound waves make the eardrum vibrate, the ossicles transmit these movements to the oval window and into the inner ear.

ardrum is a hin membrane etween the outer nd middle parts f the ear

Cochlear nerve carries signals to the brain

Cochlea

Cochlear nerve

Sound vibrations

Hair cells

Oval window is the entrance to the inner ear

Cross-section of the cochlea

When sound vibrations reach the fluid-filled **inner ear**, they bend the "hairs" on sensory cells inside the coiled cochlea. This triggers signals that are carried by the cochlear nerve to the brain and allow us to hear sounds.

Middle ear   Inner ear

Balance

Our sense of balance allows us to stand, walk, or run without falling over. Special sensors in the inner part of each ear keep the brain updated about how upright we are and what movements the head is making.

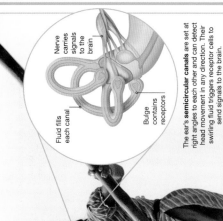

Nerve carries signals to the brain

Fluid fills each canal

Bulge contains receptors

The ear's **semicircular canals** are set at right angles to each other and can detect head movement in any direction. Their swirling fluid triggers receptor cells to send signals to the brain.

Staying upright

There are three semicircular canals inside the ear that are filled with fluid. They contain balance sensors that detect body movements and send signals to the brain. These signals, together with signals from our eyes, pressure sensors in the skin on our feet, and stretch sensors in our muscles, are processed by the brain. The brain instructs the muscles to adjust the body's position so that it stays upright and balanced.

When you are in an elevator, your ear sensors tell your brain whether you are going up or down.

An acrobat balances as she moves across a tightrope

Feeling dizzy

Spinning around, such as on a amusement park ride, makes people feel dizzy. That is because sensors in the ears' semicircular canals send confusing information to the brain. This confusion can also cause motion sickness during a bumpy ride in a car, plane, or boat.

Chemical messengers

In addition to the nervous system, the body has a second control system—the endocrine system. This releases hormones into the bloodstream. Hormones are chemical messengers that target specific body tissues and change the way they act. They control growth, reproduction, and many other processes.

Making hormones

This body map shows some of the endocrine glands that release hormones and make up the endocrine system. Some, such as the pituitary, thyroid, and adrenal glands, only release hormones. Some also have other functions—for example, the kidneys also filter the blood and make urine.

The **adrenal gland** releases epinephrine, which prepares the body to deal with danger

The **pancreas** releases two hormones that control blood sugar levels

The **pituitary gland** releases nine hormones

The **thyroid gland** releases two hormones

Kidneys release renin, which helps control blood pressure

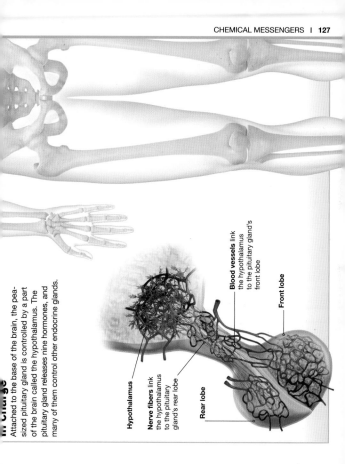

Attached to the base of the brain, the pea-sized pituitary gland is controlled by a part of the brain called the hypothalamus. The pituitary gland releases nine hormones, and many of them control other endocrine glands.

Hypothalamus

Nerve fibers link the hypothalamus to the pituitary gland's rear lobe

Rear lobe

Blood vessels link the hypothalamus to the pituitary gland's front lobe

Front lobe

Hormones in action

There are more than 50 hormones in the body. Each controls a different activity, such as reacting to danger, triggering growth, and managing fuel supplies for energy.

Hormone rush

The hormone epinephrine is released to help people face or flee from danger. This fast-acting hormone increases the heart and breathing rates, fuel supply, and blood flow to the muscles.

Growing up

Released by the pituitary gland, growth hormone (GH) makes a child's bones grow longer. Growth happens when new bone tissue is added at the ends of bones. Bones stop growing in adults.

Free-fall skydiving is exciting but scary and causes a rush of epinephrine

X-ray showing a child's hand bones

X-ray showing an adult's hand bones

Epinephrine makes our pupils wider so we can see more clearly where danger threatens.

Glucose control

The hormone insulin controls the level of glucose—the body's fuel—in the blood. People with diabetes produce very little insulin themselves and have to inject the hormone to keep their glucose levels normal.

Injecting insulin

Reproduction and growth

Every child grows from a fertilized egg
that contains body-building instructions
inherited from both parents. This egg divides
to produce trillions of cells that make up
a baby growing inside its mother's body,
like the one shown here. After it is born,
the baby passes through a series of life
stages that take it to adulthood and,
eventually, old age.

DNA
Our cells contain
DNA—two spiral strands
twisted around each other.
This substance holds the
instructions for creating
a human being.

Female and male

The reproductive system is the only body system that is different for males and females. From the teenage years onward, the male and female systems each release special sex cells—sperm in males and eggs in females—that join together to make a baby.

Male reproductive system

The male sex organs are made up of two testes and the penis on the outside of the body, and the tubes and glands that link them inside. Millions of sperm are made in the testes, carried through the tubes, and released through the penis.

A **sperm cell** is about 0.002 in (0.05 mm) long, but most of this is made up of a whiplike tail.

The **prostate gland** releases fluid that helps to protect sperm

Bladder

Tube carries sperm from the testis to the penis

The **urethra** releases sperm and also carries urine from the bladder

Each **testis**, or testicle, makes sperm

Penis

Head carries genetic information

Middle section provides energy for movement

Tail beats to move the sperm

Female reproductive system

The female sex organs are made up of the two ovaries and fallopian tubes, the uterus, and the vagina. An egg is released from one of the ovaries every month. If the egg is fertilized by a sperm, it will travel to the uterus, or womb, and develop into a baby.

An **egg, or ovum**, is the body's widest cell—0.004 in (0.1 mm) across, which is 50 times wider than the head of a sperm.

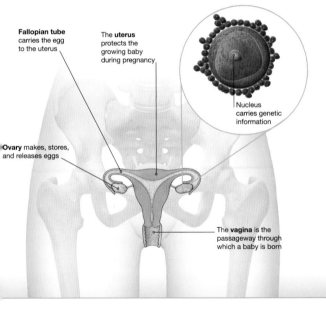

Fallopian tube carries the egg to the uterus

The **uterus** protects the growing baby during pregnancy

Nucleus carries genetic information

Ovary makes, stores, and releases eggs

The **vagina** is the passageway through which a baby is born

Fertilization

To make a baby, an egg must be fertilized by a sperm within 24 hours of being released from the ovary. Genetic information in the sperm and egg combine to form the full set of instructions needed to build a new human being.

Funnel channels the egg into the fallopian tube

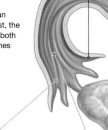

Ovary releases an egg

Building cells

The fertilized egg travels to the uterus along a fallopian tube. As it does, the egg divides again and again. First, the single cell divides into two cells, then those two cells both divide, and so on. Eventually, the tiny ball of cells reaches the uterus, or womb, and settles in its lining.

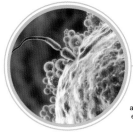

About **36 hours** after fertilization, the egg divides to form two new cells. These continue to divide every 12 hours.

Fertilization happens when a sperm penetrates the egg's outer layer (above), loses its tail, and fuses with the egg's nucleus.

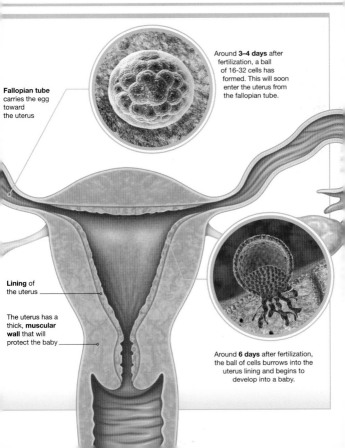

Fallopian tube carries the egg toward the uterus

Around **3–4 days** after fertilization, a ball of 16-32 cells has formed. This will soon enter the uterus from the fallopian tube.

Lining of the uterus

The uterus has a thick, **muscular wall** that will protect the baby

Around **6 days** after fertilization, the ball of cells burrows into the uterus lining and begins to develop into a baby.

In the womb

A baby grows, protected and cared for, within its mother's uterus, or womb. Over a period of nine months, known as pregnancy, a tiny ball of cells develops into a human being ready to be born.

From embryo to fetus

For the first eight weeks, the developing baby is called an embryo, and after that it is a fetus. It is protected in a bag of fluid and receives food and oxygen through the umbilical cord and placenta.

The **umbilical cord** links the baby to the placenta

The **placenta** links the umbilical cord to the mother's blood supply

At **5 weeks**, the bean-sized embryo's heart is beating and other organs are developing. Budlike limbs are starting to grow.

At **8 weeks**, the strawberry-sized fetus has a recognizable face. Its head and brain grow rapidly, and bones start to form.

Fetus measures **18 in (46 cm)**

At **11 weeks**, the lemon-sized fetus is active and uses its muscles to move its limbs. All internal organs are in place.

At **35 weeks**, a layer of fat under the skin makes the fetus plumper. It responds to sounds and light and turns head-down, ready for birth.

At **38–40 weeks**, the baby is fully developed and ready to take its first breath when it is born.

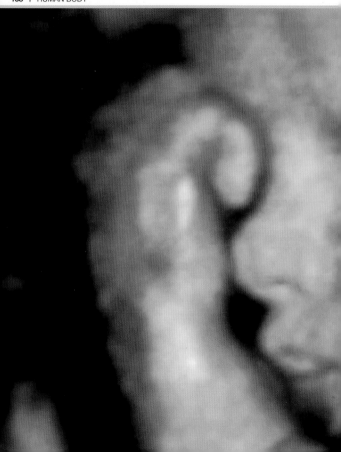

Growing babies start to dream about 12 weeks

before they are born

IN THE WOMB

With its fingers curled into a fist, this 30-week-old fetus is nearing full development as it grows inside its mother's womb. This 3-D ultrasound scan clearly shows an eye, nose, lips, and other features of the face.

Genes and DNA

Every cell in your body contains the instructions needed to build and run the body. These instructions, which are inherited from your mother and father, are called genes. The 23,000 genes in each cell are made from a substance called DNA.

Chromosome

Set of instructions

Inside a cell's nucleus, there are 46 X-shaped structures called chromosomes, each made from coiled-up DNA. DNA is made up of two strands linked by pairs of chemicals called bases. These are the "letters" that spell out the instructions in genes.

Bases link the strands, like rungs on a ladder

If the DNA in your cells were put end-to-end it would reach to the Sun and back around 600 times.

One of the two **strands** that make up DNA

The four types of **base** are shown in different colors

Passing on genes

The genes that are passed on from parents to their children control the children's features, such as the color of their eyes. Like most genes, eye-color genes have different versions. This explains why there are different eye colors.

Identical genes

Identical twins look the same because they share identical genes. This happens when a single fertilized egg splits inside the mother's womb, creating two separate cells that develop into two identical babies.

Growing up

Throughout life, everyone goes through the same stages of growth and development. The biggest changes happen between birth and the late teens—from a baby totally reliant on its parents to an independent young adult.

Early years

Infancy, childhood, and adolescence are years of great change. During this time, the brain develops very quickly, making new connections that enable us to communicate, move, and behave in more sophisticated ways. The body also changes in appearance, eventually taking on the shape and size of an adult body.

The first year of life is called **infancy**. An infant grows rapidly and progresses from lying to sitting to crawling, then standing up, and finally walking. Infants grasp objects and interact with people using sounds and facial expressions.

During **childhood**, between the ages of one and 10, the proportions of a child's body change, with limbs growing longer. The brain develops rapidly and children learn to speak and read, run and jump, and pick up life skills.

The change from a child to an adult, called **adolescence**, happens during our teenage years. In addition to the physical changes of puberty, this phase includes changes in behavior, emotions, and attitudes. These are triggered by changes in the hormones and in the brain.

PUBERTY

The first part of adolescence is puberty. The body grows rapidly and changes shape, and the reproductive system becomes active. Because puberty starts earlier in girls (age 10 to 12) than boys (age 12 to 14), girls initially grow faster than boys.

Adulthood and old age

At about the age of 20, the body stops growing and we enter adulthood. But the adult body continues to change, and gradually signs of aging begin to appear.

In **middle age**, between the ages of 40 and 60, the first signs of aging appear. Many organs become less efficient, including bones that are weaker and muscles that are less powerful. The brain, however, often works better than ever.

Young adults between the ages of 20 and 40 are at the peak of fitness, health, and fertility (the ability to have children).

Old age, from 60 onward, is when signs of aging become more obvious. Hair thins and turns gray, sight and hearing become less efficient, muscles weaken and joints stiffen, and bones break more easily.

Aging skin
The most obvious visible sign of aging is wrinkled skin, often with brown age spots. With age, the skin's dermis (the layer under the surface) becomes thinner and looser, with deeper creases.

Wrinkles

Age spots

Dermis becomes thinner

This cross-section of the **skin** of an older person shows the effects of aging. Age spots occur where skin is exposed to the Sun.

Your amazing body

CELLS

★ The body's biggest cells—female egg cells—are ⁴⁄₁₀₀₀ in (0.1 mm) **across** and visible to the naked eye.

★ Lined up in a row, **40 average-sized cells** would stretch across a period.

★ **300 million body cells** die and are replaced every minute.

★ Liver cells last for about **18 months**.

★ Red blood cells can last for up to **120 days**.

★ Small intestine cells last for just **36 hours** before they are worn away by the passage of food.

SKIN, NAILS, AND HAIR

• The outer layer of the skin, the upper epidermis, is replaced **every month**.

• About **50,000 skin flakes** drop off the skin's surface every minute. That amounts to about 40 lb (20 kg) of skin flakes in a lifetime, which is about the weight of a young child.

• Skin varies in thickness, from ²⁄₁₀₀ in (0.5 mm) on the eyelids to ¼ in (6 mm) on the soles of the feet.

• The skin is the body's heaviest organ, weighing about **11 lb (5 kg)** in an adult.

• Skin color depends on the amount of pigment or **melanin** that the skin produces. Small amounts of melanin result in light skin, while large amounts result in dark skin.

• Each human being has around **2.5 million sweat pores**. Sweat empties through the pores onto the skin's surface.

• Fingernails **grow four times faster** than toenails, and faster in summer than in winter.

• **About 120 head hairs** (out of 100,000 in total) are lost and replaced daily.

• Head hair normally grows ½ in (12 mm) a month. It usually stops growing when it is 2 ft (60 cm) long, falls out, and is replaced. Some people, however, can grow their hair to 13 ft (4 m) long.

• Nearly everyone has **eyelash mites** (harmless, sausage-shaped animals) that live in the hair follicles of humans.

BONES AND MUSCLES

◆ A newborn baby has more than 300 bones, but as the baby grows some bones fuse together to form larger bones. An adult's skeleton is made up of **206 bones**.

◆ The skeleton makes up around **20 percent of an adult's body weight**.

◆ The body's longest bone—the femur (thighbone)—is **150 times longer** than the smallest—the stirrup bone inside the ear.

◆ The hands contain more than **one-quarter of the body's bones**.

◆ Bones may seem to be dry but are actually **22 percent water**.

◆ We use at least **12 face muscles** while smiling and 11 for frowning.

◆ An average person walks about **80,000 miles (128,000 km)** in a lifetime—the same distance as walking around the world three times.

◆ The bulkiest muscle in the body is the **gluteus maximus** in each buttock, used for powerful actions such as climbing stairs.

HEART AND BLOOD

★ Blood makes up about **8 percent of our body weight**.

★ The heart pumps around **10½ pints (5 liters)** of blood around the body every minute. Each day it pumps enough blood to fill 170 bathtubs.

★ The average length of a capillary is **⁴⁄₁₀₀ in (1 mm)**.

★ Spread out flat, the enormous network of capillaries—which deliver oxygen to body cells—would cover an **area the size of 19 tennis courts**.

More than 10 billion white blood cells are produced daily to destroy invading bacteria.

URINARY SYSTEM

• In an average lifetime, the urinary system makes and releases around **70,000 pints (40,000 liters)** of urine—enough to fill a small swimming pool.

• Every day, around **380 pints (180 liters)** of fluid are filtered from blood by the kidneys, but only 3 pints (1.5 liters) of waste leave the body as urine.

• The kidneys make up just **1 percent of the body's weight** but consume 25 percent of its energy.

BREATHING

♦ On average, we breathe in and out around **30,000 times a day**—exhaling enough air to inflate 3,750 party balloons.

♦ **Inhaled air** contains 20.8 percent oxygen, 0.04 percent carbon dioxide, and 79.16 percent nitrogen. Exhaled air contains 15.6 percent oxygen, 4 percent carbon dioxide, 79.16 percent nitrogen, and 1.24 percent water vapor.

♦ Every day, we swallow a large glassful of **slimy mucus**, which is produced by the airways, pushed up to the throat, and swallowed back into the esophagus.

DIGESTION

★ The salivary glands release around **4.2 pints (2 liters) of saliva** into the mouth every day.

★ The **gastric juice** released by the stomach is so acidic that it can strip paint.

★ **Tooth enamel** contains no living cells. If it is damaged, it cannot be replaced, except by fillings.

★ We have **two sets of teeth in a lifetime**: 20 baby (deciduous) teeth in childhood, which are replaced by up to 32 permanent adult teeth.

BRAIN

• The brain is about **90 percent water**.

• A new-born baby's brain weighs about ⅚ lb (375 g) but triples in size and weight to 2.2 lb (1 kg) by the infant's first birthday.

• The brain makes up **2 percent of the body's weight** but receives 20 percent of the body's blood supply.

• Spread out, the **cerebral cortex**—the thin outer layer of the cerebrum which forms the "thinking" part of the brain—would cover the same area as a large pillow case.

• The **right side** of the brain controls the left side of the body and the left side of the brain controls the right side of the body.

• Over **250 million nerve fibers** link the left and right sides of the brain.

• Every day, adults between the ages of 20 and 60 lose about **12,000 brain neurons** that are never replaced.

• Brain neurons can last for up to **100 years**—a whole lifetime for most people.

NERVES AND NEURONS

✦ A nerve impulse (signal) takes just **one hundredth of a second** to travel from the spinal cord to your big toe.

✦ The longest neurons—between spinal cord and big toes—are **3¼ ft (1 m) long**. They are also the longest cells in the body. The shortest neurons are ⁴⁄₁₀₀ in (1 mm) long.

✦ A neuron can transmit **1,000 nerve impulses** every second.

✦ The widest nerve, the sciatic, is **¾ in (2 cm) wide**. It extends from the lower back to the foot.

✦ A withdrawal reflex—when a nerve signal passes through the spinal cord, not the brain—can pull the hand away from a dangerously hot object in just **30 thousandths of a second (30 milliseconds)**. If the signal went via the brain it would take 800 milliseconds.

✦ Stretched out, the body's nerves would extend for more than **93,000 miles (150,000 km)**—more than the distance covered by flying between London and New York 25 times.

SENSES

★ Our **hearing range decreases with age**, which is why young people hear higher-pitched sounds than older people.

★ The tongue's **taste buds** are replaced every week, but the nose's smell receptors last for a month.

★ Chiles "taste" hot because they contain a substance that triggers the **tongue's pain receptors**.

★ Fingers are among the **most sensitive areas** of the body. Each fingertip has about 100 touch receptors.

★ The eyes contain **70 percent of the body's sensory receptors**, making sight our most important sense.

★ Eyelids blink about **9,400 times** a day, helping to keep our eyes clean.

The farthest object that we see without a telescope is the Andromeda galaxy, which is 2.5 million light-years away.

GENES

• Humans have **46 gene-carrying chromosomes** inside the nucleus of each body cell.

• Stretched out, the DNA in one human cell would extend over **6½ ft (2 m)**.

Glossary

Artery A thick-walled blood vessel that carries blood from the heart to the tissues.

Axon A long fiber that extends from the cell body of a neuron and carries signals to other nerve cells.

Bacteria A group of small, single-celled microorganisms, some of which cause disease in humans.

Bone marrow A soft tissue found in the spaces within bones.

Calcium A mineral used by the body to build bones and teeth.

Capillary A microscopic blood vessel that links the smallest arteries to the smallest veins, and delivers blood to tissue cells.

Carbohydrate A group of substances found in food and inside the body. It includes sugars, such as glucose—the body's store of energy.

Carbon dioxide A gas that is the waste product of energy release inside cells.

Cardiac Of or relating to the heart.

Cartilage A tough, flexible tissue that helps support the body and covers the ends of bones in joints.

Cell One of the trillions of microscopic living units that make up the body.

Chromosome One of 46 packages of DNA found in the nucleus of each cell.

Chyme A creamy liquid that is produced by the part-digestion of food in the stomach.

Cilia Tiny hairlike structures found on some tissue. They wave to move things, such as mucus, across their surface.

Collagen A tough protein that makes up the fibers that strengthen tendons, ligaments, and cartilage.

CT (computed tomography) scan A method of producing 2-D and 3-D images of body tissues and organs.

Cytoplasm The jellylike fluid found between the membrane and nucleus of a cell.

Dendrite A short fiber that carries incoming signals from other nerve cells to the cell body of a neuron.

Dermis The deeper, thicker layer of skin, below the epidermis. It contains sensory receptors and blood vessels.

Digestion The process by which food is broken down into simple nutrients that can be absorbed into the bloodstream and used by the body.

Digestive enzyme A substance that speeds up the breakdown of food molecules.

DNA (deoxyribonucleic acid) A long molecule found inside the nucleus of body cells. It contains the coded instructions needed to build and run a body.

Embryo A developing baby between the time it arrives in the uterus and eight weeks after fertilization.

Energy The fuel that comes from eating food. It is essential for keeping the body's cells working and alive.

Enzyme A protein that speeds up chemical reactions inside the body.

Epidermis The thin protective layer of the skin.

Fat A group of substances found in food and inside the body. Fat stores energy and insulates the body.

Fertilization The joining together of a male sperm and a female egg to make a new human being.

Fetus The name given to baby from the ninth week after fertilization until birth.

Gastric Of or relating to the stomach.

Gene One of 23,000 coded instructions stored in the DNA that makes up the chromosomes inside a cell's nucleus.

Germ A common name given to microorganisms that cause disease.

Gland A group of cells that make and release specific substances such as hormones and enzymes.

Glucose A type of sugar found in the bloodstream that is the main source of energy for body cells.

Hemoglobin A red, oxygen-carrying protein found inside red blood cells.

Hepatic Of or relating to the liver.

Hormone A chemical messenger released by the endocrine glands into the bloodstream. It alters the activities of specific tissues.

Immune system A collection of cells, including macrophages and lymphocytes, that protect the body from disease by destroying germs such as bacteria.

Joint The place where two or more bones meet. Most joints are movable.

Keratin A tough, waterproof protein found in nails, hair, and the upper layer of the skin's epidermis.

Ligament A tough strap that holds bones together at the joints.

Lymph A liquid that is drained from the body's tissues along the vessels of the lymphatic system.

Mammal An animal, such as a rabbit or human, that is warm-blooded, hairy, and feeds its young with milk.

Metabolism All the chemical processes that take place inside every one of the body's cell.

Mitochondria The tiny structures inside cells that release energy from glucose.

Mitosis The division of a body cell into two new, identical offspring cells.

MRI (magnetic resonance imaging) scan A way of using magnetism, radio waves, and computers to produce images of body tissues and organs.

Mucus A slimy substance released by glands, such as those lining the esophagus that leads from the throat to the stomach.

Muscle fiber One of the cells that makes up a muscle.

Neuron A type of nerve cell that carries signals.

Nucleus The control center of the cell that contains chromosomes.

Nutrient A substance found in food that is needed by the body to function normally.

Organ A body part, such as the heart or kidney, that is made of two or more types of tissue and has specific roles.

Organelle One of the tiny working structures, such as mitochondria, found floating in the cytoplasm of cells.

Oxygen A gas that is used by body cells to release energy from glucose.

Protein A group of substances found in food and inside the body. Proteins build and run the body's cells.

Puberty The period of rapid growth, usually in the early teens, when the reproductive systems start working.

Pulse The rhythmic throbbing of an artery as it expands when blood is pumped through it by the heart. The pulse is the same as the rate the heart beats.

Reflex A rapid, automatic action, such as pulling the hand away from a hot object, that happens without our thinking about it.

Renal Of or relating to the kidney.

Saliva A liquid found in the mouth. It aids digestion by providing the lubrication needed for chewing and swallowing.

SEM (scanning electron microscopy) A way of using a special microscope to produce magnified 3-D images of body tissue.

Sphincter A ring of muscle around an opening that controls the flow of materials through it.

Sweat A watery liquid produced by glands in the skin.

Synapse The junction between two neurons that are separated by a tiny gap.

Synovial joint A free-moving joint, such as the elbow or knee.

System A group of linked organs that work together, such as the organs that make up the digestive system

Tendon A tough cord that links a muscle to a bone.

Tissue A group of cells of the same type—such as muscle cells—that work together to perform a particular function.

Vein A thin-walled blood vessel that returns blood to the heart from the tissues.

Virus A disease-causing particle that invades the body's cells and multiplies inside them, causing infections, such as colds and measles.

X-ray An imaging technique that uses radiation to reveal bones.

Index

Acknowledgments

Dorling Kindersley would like to thank: Lorrie Mack for proofreading; Helen Peters for indexing; Joe Fullman and Catherine Saunders for editorial assistance; and Vikas Chauhan for design assistance.

The publisher would like to thank the following for their kind permission to reproduce their photographs:

(Key: a-above; b-below/bottom; c-center; f-far; l-left; r-right; t-top)

1 Science Photo Library: Gustoimages. **2–3 Corbis:** Dennis Kunkel Microscopy, Inc. / Visuals Unlimited. **4 Corbis:** Isaac Lane Koval (cl). **4–5 Corbis:** Michael Keller. **5 Corbis:** Ton Koene / Visuals Unlimited (br). **Dreamstime.com:** Jacek Chabraszewski (tr). **6 Alamy Images:** Phototake Inc. (bc). **7 Corbis:** Dennis Kunkel Microscopy, Inc. / Visuals Unlimited (tr). **8–9 Fotolia:** martanfoto. **11 Getty Images:** Image Source (tr); Michel Tcherevkoff / Stone (l). **13 Getty Images:** Zephyr / Science Photo Library (ca). **14 Corbis:** Dan McCoy— Rainbow / Science Faction (br). **Dreamstime.com:** Peterfactors (cl). **15 Corbis:** Photo Quest Ltd. / Science Photo Library (br); Zephyr / Science Photo Library (cr). **Getty Images:** UHB Trust / Stone (cra); BSIP / Universal Images Group (bl). **16–17 Corbis:** Image Source. **22–23 Science Photo Library:** Steve Gschmeissner. **23 Fotolia:** Aaron Amat (tr). **24 Corbis:** Scientifica / Visuals Unlimited. **25 Getty Images:** Sam Jordash / Digital Vision (tl); Michael Krasowitz / Taxi (br). **28–29 Corbis:** Photo Quest Ltd. / Science Photo Library. **30 Corbis:** Steve Gschmeissner / Science Photo Library (bc). **31 Corbis:** Dennis Kunkel Microscopy, Inc. / Visuals Unlimited (bc); Lester V. Bergman (cr). **33**

Corbis: Ralph Hutchings / Visuals Unlimited (cb). **35 Corbis:** ERproductions Ltd. / Blend Images (tl). **Dreamstime.com:** Fotokon (tr). **37 Corbis:** Kallista Images / Visuals Unlimited (l). **42 Corbis:** Mediscan (clb). **43 Corbis:** Carolina Biological / Visuals Unlimited (tr); Steve Gschmeissner / Science Photo Library (br). **46–47 Corbis:** Dennis Kunkel Microscopy, Inc. / Visuals Unlimited. **50 Fotolia:** michelangelus. **56–57 Corbis:** Science Picture Co / Science Faction. **58 Science Photo Library:** Susumu Nishinaga (bc). **59 Corbis:** Howard Sochurek (r). **61 Dreamstime.com:** Calisto65 (tl); Corbis (tl). **68–69 Corbis:** Dr. David Phillips / Visuals Unlimited. **76 Corbis:** Science Picture Co / Science Faction. **77 Alamy Images:** Enigma (cb). **78 Corbis:** Veronika Burmeister / Visuals Unlimited (ca). **79 Science Photo Library:** CNRI (tc). **85 Dreamstime.com:** Gemenacom (r). **86 Dreamstime.com:** Sebastian Kaulitzki. **87 Corbis:** Mediscan (cb). **92 Science Photo Library:** Dr. K. F. R. Schiller (b). **93 Corbis:** Micro Discovery (cl). **96–97 Science Photo Library:** Eye of Science. **100 Science Photo Library:** David McCarthy (cl). **102 Getty Images:** Jan Scherders / Blend Images. **103 Dreamstime.com:** Venki3503 (cb). **105 Getty Images:** Visuals Unlimited, Inc. / Carol & Mike Werner (cb). **108–109 Corbis:** Dennis Kunkel Microscopy, Inc. / Visuals Unlimited. **112 Getty Images:** Steve Gschmeissner / Science Photo Library (ca). **113 Science Photo Library:** BSIP, Chassenet (ca, tr). **114–115 Corbis:** Jens Nieth. **116 Dreamstime.com:** Kamil Macniak (tl). **117 Corbis:** Fabrice Lerouge / Onoky (tc). **119 Fotolia:** dragon_fang (br). **120 Corbis:** Ondrea Barbe (bc). **Dreamstime.com:** Zigf (br). **121 Corbis:** Claire Artman (br); Tom Grill (cr); Chris Whitehead / cultura (bc). **Fotolia:** April Cat (bl).

Getty Images: UIG (tl). **123 Corbis:** MedicalRF.com (tc). **124–125 Getty Images:** Sajjad Hussain / AFP (c). **125 Corbis:** RelaXimages (br). **128 Corbis:** Yoav Levy / MedNet (tbl); Visuals Unlimited (br). **128–129 Getty Images:** Oliver Furrer. **129 Getty Images:** Science Photo Library (br). **130 Getty Images:** SCIEPRO / Science Photo Library. **131 Fotolia:** adimas (bc). **137 Science Photo Library:** Jellyfish Pictures (b). **138–139 Science Photo Library:** GE Medical Systems. **141 Dreamstime.com:** Bill Warchol (b). **Fotolia:** IKO (cra). **142 Dreamstime.com:** Val Thoermer (r). **143 Corbis:** David Katzenstein / Citizen Stock (br). **144 Corbis:** Richard Lewisohn / Image Source (r). **Dreamstime.com:** Tom Wang (l). **145 Fotolia:** keki (br); Rohit Seth (l).

Jacket images: Front: Science Photo Library: Pasieka c; Spine: Science Photo Library: Pasieka t.

All other images © Dorling Kindersley

For further information see:
www.dkimages.com